M000311790

What, Then, Would You Be?

Cycle A Sermons for
Lent and Easter
Based on Second Lesson Texts

Dr. Ronald H. Love

CSS Publishing Company, Inc.
Lima, Ohio

WHAT, THEN, WOULD YOU BE?
CYCLE A SERMONS FOR LENT AND EASTER
BASED ON SECOND LESSON TEXTS

FIRST EDITION
Copyright © 2017
by CSS Publishing Co., Inc.

Library of Congress Cataloging-in-Publication Data

Names: Love, Ronald H., author.
Title: What, then, would you be? : Cycle A sermons for Lent and Easter based on second lesson texts / Dr. Ronald H. Love.
Description: First edition. | Lima, Ohio : CSS Publishing Company, Inc., [2017] | Includes bibliographical references and index.
Identifiers: LCCN 2017007730 (print) | LCCN 2017020163 (ebook) | ISBN 9780788028809 (e-book) | ISBN 0788028804 (e-book) | ISBN 9780788028793 (pbk. : alk. paper) | ISBN 0788028790 (pbk. : alk. paper)
Subjects: LCSH: Lenten sermons. | Easter--Sermons. | Bible. New Testament--Sermons. | Common lectionary (1992). Year A.
Classification: LCC BV4277 (ebook) | LCC BV4277 .L69 2017 (print) | DDC 252/.62--dc23

For more information about CSS Publishing Company resources, visit our website at www.csspub.com, email us at csr@csspub.com, or call (800) 241-4056.

e-book:
ISBN-13: 978-0-7880-2880-4
ISBN-10: 0-7880-2880-9

ISBN-13: 978-0-7880-2879-3
ISBN-10: 0-7880-2879-0

PRINTED IN USA

To my mother —
a truly angelic person

Preface

A minister has many roles to fulfill in the church. One professor I studied under listed them as three: King, prophet, priest. In the role of a king you are to administer the church. In the role of a prophet you to speak to the social issues that are confronting society. In the role of a priest you are to meet the spiritual needs of your congregation.

The United Methodist church confesses that a minister is called to Word, Sacrament, and Order. The pastor appointed to a local church is to be responsible for the Word of God, both in preaching and teaching. A part of this responsibility is that the Word of God is an orthodox expression of the scriptures. Regarding the Sacrament, only the pastor is permitted to administer the sacraments. This function of his or her office is to protect the sacredness of baptism and Holy Communion. A pastor's responsibility in maintaining the order of the church is be certain that all administrative action of the church are in compliance with the Book of Discipline.

The apostle Paul never clearly defined the role of a minister, but he did give some insight. The church has various offices when he wrote that some are called to be apostles, prophets, evangelists, pastors, and teachers. It should be understood that a minister will ascribed to each of these roles. Though Paul makes it clear that as all Christians are members of the Body of Christ, so each has a role to play, it must be realized that the minister is still the one who must oversee and coordinated that organizational structure of the church.

In all the roles outlined as the duty of the pastor, what remains paramount in the minds of parishioners is the ability to preach. As important as being a good administrator is and the comfort that a sincere pastor can bestow, a minister still seems to be judged by his or her ability to preach above all else. This may not be a fair assessment and it may be unfair for those who are great pastors but lack being dynamic pulpiters, but it is the realty that clergy must deal with.

The apostle Paul did highlight the importance of preaching when he wrote, "How, then, can they call on the one they have not believed in? And how can they believe in the one of whom they have not heard? And how can they hear without someone preaching to them?" We can think of preaching as individual witnessing, but the thrust of this message from Paul is to be actually standing before a congregation and proclaiming the good news of Jesus Christ. It is sharing the gospel message of repentance, forgiveness and salvation. It is sharing the gospel message of the hope and assurance that we have from believing in Jesus. It is the gospel message that articulates that a Christian is kind, gentle, caring, and compassionate. A single sermon may not contain all of these elements, but in the course of the Christian year each of these topics must be highlighted.

The apostle Paul went on to write, "And how can anyone preach unless they are sent? As it is written: 'How beautiful are the feet of those who bring good news!' " If we are called and then sent to preach the good news, then we must take that mandate seriously. This means that sermon preparation cannot be a Saturday night message that is hastily scratched on a dinner table napkin; but, it must be a composition that is carefully crafted days, weeks, and even months in advance of its delivery.

In developing my sermons, I use what I call the 5Es as an outline for sermon preparation and delivery. The 5Es are as follow:

E = Enlighten: The sermon must spiritually enrich the congregation. The sermon must present the scriptures and theology in a format that is easily comprehended and applied. It must be felt by the congregation that through the presentation they are being drawn closer to God and have a better understanding of themselves and the meaning and purpose of life. Individuals will stop attending a sermon that leaves one despondent as opposed to being lifted up to the throne of God.

E = Educate: The congregation must feel that they have learned something new from the sermon. They must feel the personal investment of their time was profitable for the information received gave them a better understanding of complementary academic disciplines and life events.

E = Entertain: The presentation must be interesting and enjoyable to listen to. The attention of the congregation must be maintained or communication ceases. The mind of bored recipients will drift and eventually be lost altogether. Entertaining is not devoid of meaning, because it is an integral aspect of understanding. Illustrations function as the stained-glass windows in a church sanctuary. Windows of clear glass bring the light of the message that is unfiltered and blinding. A message that is that is seen through stained-glass takes on soft and beautiful hues. A sermon that is blended in the color of stained-glass, rather than being a blinding diatribe through unfiltered clear glass, would enhance the sermon's meaning and promotes its ability to be both listened to and understood. A sermon must have meaningful illustrations to foster comprehension and maintain the attention of the congregation.

E = Enthusiasm: The preacher must be excited about the material and this joy must be conveyed to the congregation. The preacher must be animated, displaying how important the topic under discussion is for him or her. The excitement of the congregation cannot rise above that of the presenter. Enthusiasm underscores that the message is relevant and important, and the preacher desires the audience to share in his or her excitement. Enthusiasm is contagious. If the parishioners who are listening to the discourse and are not enthralled, then they will not remain engaged and feel that the topic is insignificant for their daily living.

E = Encourage: The sermon must challenge the congregation to action. The message must encourage the congregation to become intentional in their endeavors in implementing the sermon's call for action. It is imperative that the congregation is able to apply the message to their current life situation.

Every minister has his or her own style for sermon preparation. Though there are many factors that contribute to that process, the overriding factor is that a pastor develops a method that suits his or her personality. Therefore, I offer my 5Es only as a way for the reader to reexamine his or her present style of sermon preparation, and adopt and adapt any aspect that I present as it compliments your individual personality.

I want to thank you for taking the time to read the sermons in this book, What, then, would you be? It is my prayer and my hope that the sermons are profitable for your use.

Dr. Ronald H. Love
Florence, South Carolina
February 1, 2017

Table Of Contents

In this sermon series, when the sermon refers to a "friend" in the text, it actually refers to the author of the sermon, Dr. Ronald H. Love.

What, Then, Would You Be?

John Quincy Adams, the sixth president of the United States, was an enthusiastic swimmer. Before starting each day's work he would swim and bathe naked in the Potomac River. There was a newspaper woman, Anne Royall, who tried for weeks to get an interview with the president, but she was always rebuffed. One day she followed Adams to his watering hole. After he disrobed and got into the river, she promptly sat down on his clothes. Recognizing who she was, Adams pleaded, "Let me get out and dress, and I swear you shall have your interview." Royall was unconvinced of the sincerity behind the remark and remained seated. When the president still refused to answer questions posed to him, Royall threatened to scream if Adams attempted to get out of the water. This would summon nearby fishermen around the bend of the river. While President Adams remained discreetly submerged in the water, Anne Royall got her exclusive interview.

We are the newspaper reporters of this day and we have a remarkable story of good news to share with family, friends, neighbors, coworkers, and anyone whom we may encounter that may be receptive to listening. It is the story of Jesus Christ and his message of forgiveness, healing, equality, and genuinely caring about others. Sometimes people will patiently listen to us and other times we may just to have to sit on their clothes to get them to pause long enough to listen; but, in either case with determination and sincerity we share the gospel message.

Paul wrote to the church in Corinth specifically referring to himself as an ambassador. The Corinthian Christians were under the domain of the Roman Empire so they were well aware of the implications of Paul calling himself an ambassador. In Roman provinces the emperor would appoint a legate, an ambassador, to represent him. This is a very powerful and influential position for a legate speaks "on behalf of" or "in place of" the emperor himself. The legate speaks with the authority of the emperor himself.

In using this analogy Paul is professing that he is an ambassador for Jesus Christ to the church. Paul in his message to the Corinthians is speaking "on behalf of" or "in place of" Jesus. It is Paul's intent that his message is taken seriously.

Paul's message is the Corinthians must reconcile themselves to Jesus and to one another, once again taking their faith seriously.

Since Paul's last visit to the church a number of problems arose. Some of the Christians began to worship the foreign god Aphrodite, the goddess of love. Some of the Christians began to live a life of debauchery. And within the church itself there were factions that were causing disruptions.

So Paul's message of reconciliation was very understandable, clear, and forthright. The Corinthian Christians must return to the devout and holy life that once prevailed among them. The Corinthian Christians must reconcile themselves to both God and each other.

Paul then wrote about his own life as a way to demonstrate and encourage the Corinthians to return to righteous living. Paul did not pen these words out of arrogance or egocentricity, but he wrote them as an ambassador. He wrote them as one who wanted to demonstrate what it meant to live as a representative of Jesus. Paul wrote about how he endured undue hardships and sacrifice for the sake of proclaiming the gospel message. With Paul's story, on this Ash Wednesday, we see ashes symbolically placed upon his forehead.

The use of ashes is a significant ritual in Judaism. It begins with the transgression of Adam where we get the ritualistic words that accompany our practice this day. In Genesis we read, "Remember that you are dust, and to dust you shall return." Beyond Genesis ashes continue to be a symbolic representation of reconciliation. In Second Samuel when Tamar was raped by her half-brother, she sprinkled ashes on her head to express her grief. Job placed ashes upon himself to express sorrow for his sins and faults. Jeremiah called the Israelites to repentance calling them to "gird on sackcloth, roll in ashes." Daniel pleaded with God saying, "I turned to the Lord God, pleading in earnest prayer, with fasting, sackcloth and ashes." Jesus even made reference to this Jewish practice of repentance. When the inhabitants of two cities who witnessed the miracles of Jesus and yet refused to repent Jesus said unto them, "If the mighty works done in you had been done in Tyre and Sidon, they would have repented long ago sitting in sackcloth and ashes."

The early church continued this practice. Ash Wednesday begins the liturgical season of Lent which lasts forty days, representative of the forty days Jesus spent in the desert enduring the temptations of Satan. In the early church on Ash Wednesday those Christians who committed grave faults were forced to wear sackcloth and be sprinkled with ashes. They were turned out of the Christian community the same as when Adam was turned out of the Garden of Eden. During these forty days they were to reflect and do penance. On Maundy Thursday, the day we celebrate the Passover meal and the Lord's Supper, they were allowed once again back into the Christian community, reconciled with the Lord and with their brothers and sisters in Christ. Ash Wednesday was for the church a time for reflection, repentance, and reconciliation.

In the year 1091 at the Synod of Beneventum, Pope Urban II made the receiving of ashes on the forehead a common practice for all Christians. Up to this time the practice was referred to by the Latin term *dies cinerum* or "day of ashes." At the synod it was officially called in Latin as Feria Quarta Cinerum or "Ash Wednesday," as we call it today.

Paul's message to the Corinthian Christians was that they needed to reflect on their lives of apostasy and once again be reconciled to the Lord and to one another within the Christian community.

On the forehead of Paul we can see the sign of the cross made with the ashes from the burning of palms from the previous year's Palm Sunday celebration. We can see a man of reflection who preached reconciliation. For this reason Paul could lift up his life as a legate, as an ambassador, as a spokesperson for Jesus, to guide others in faithful obedience to the gospel message. Paul did this by sharing nine sufferings he had endured and eight virtues that he had practiced.

Often by listening to the life story of another individual, and especially the hardships they have overcome, our own lives can be transformed.

Johnny Cash, having once himself been in prison, made it his mission that throughout his career he would sing in penitentiaries, hoping his life story and the words of his songs would reconcile others to the good life. On New Year's Day he performed in San Quentin Penitentiary, and there was an inmate in the audience who heard his message. The early years of this inmate were spent living in a house that his father fashioned from an abandoned refrigerated railroad car. When he was nine years old his father died, throwing his world into chaos. Two years later he hopped his first railroad car and began a life of crime. In 1958 he was sentenced to San Quentin for burglary. This inmate dabbled in singing and playing the guitar prior to prison, but after hearing Johnny Cash, the year was 1959 or 1960, we don't know which, he vowed to make music his life's ambition. Upon his release from prison, he pursued his dream and became one of the greatest country-western singers of all time, with 38 number one country hits. That inmate's name was Merle Haggard.

By hearing the story of another person who found redemption we too can be reconciled to the good life. This was

Paul's hope in sharing his story with the Corinthian Christians.

Paul listed nine sufferings that he endured for the sake of the gospel. These are: afflictions, hardships, calamities, beatings, imprisonments, riots, labors, sleepless nights, and hunger. He placed these before the Corinthians asking if they were willing to make the same sacrifices. Paul was asking if they would surrender the worship of false gods to accept the challenge of obedience to the gospel message. Paul was asking if they would stop quarreling among themselves, and act in unity for the evangelistic mission of the church. Paul is asking us how we will answer these questions today.

We fortunately have not encountered many of the same sufferings as Paul. Prison and beatings are not a worry for us. But, have we had a sleepless night wondering if we could have done more, done better? Have we labored for the sake of the gospel to the point of exhaustion?

Ash Wednesday is the beginning of Lent and the season for self-examination. Are we going to be commanded to put on sackcloth and be cast out of the fellowship until Maundy Thursday because of an uncaring disposition — because we quarrel — because we refuse to compromise — because we are selfish — because we don't take every opportunity we have to share the gospel message? Lent is the season of the Christian year for self-reflection. What is your answer?

It can be hoped that upon reflection and with the reorientation of our priorities that we will be found to be faithful and obedient servants. It can be hoped that it will be found that we are willing to be reconciled to one another and to our Savior. It can be hoped that at the conclusion the season of Lent we will find that instead of sackcloth we will be wearing the white robe of martyrdom.

Instead of condemning the Corinthian Christians, Paul offered them hope. It is the hope that comes from the indwelling of the Holy Spirit that can guide and enrich us. It is the Spirit of reconciliation. When we open ourselves to the

Holy Spirit Paul offers eight attributes that it bestows upon us. These are: purity, knowledge, patience, kindness, holiness of spirit, genuine love, truthful speech, and the power of God. What a contrast to the quarrelling and bickering and disobedience presently abounding in the church in Corinth. Is it a contrast or a representation of your life this day?

If we don't want to find ourselves wearing sackcloth this Lenten season but instead be active and contributing members of the Body of Christ, the church, then we must focus on these gifts of the Holy Spirit. It is through fasting, which we are supposed to do every Friday during Lent, prayer, private devotions, participating in small groups, and public worship that we open our hearts and souls to the indwelling of God's presence.

It is through spiritual discipline, which is the hallmark of Lent, that we become pure in mind and heart. It is how we gain knowledge and learn patience. It is how kindness and genuine love become a part of our normal disposition. It is how we are reconciled to friend and stranger alike. It is how we are reconciled to our brothers and sisters in Christ who sit among us in this sanctuary. It is how we are reconciled with our Lord and Savior Jesus Christ.

Marin De Boylesve was a nineteenth-century French Jesuit priest. He wrote a meditation for each day of the year. He arranged his meditations following the church's liturgical calendar. In 1877 they were published with the title *A Thought for Each Day of the Year*. In one meditation he reflected on Jesus' teaching of a hireling or a shepherd watching over the sheep, protecting them from the wolf. The wolf, De Boylesve wrote, represents evil that draws a person to vice. The hireling follows the wolf for he has no love for souls. Then there is the good shepherd who stands fast against the wolf, remaining obedient and faithful. De Boylesve ends his meditation by asking, "What, then, would you be?" A hireling or a shepherd?

What, then, would you be?

Smombies

Joseph Chamblin was lost, and then he was found.

In 2011, Chamblin was lost. He was a staff sergeant in the United States Marines and one of the four snipers court-martialed for urinating on the fresh corpses of Taliban fighters in Afghanistan.

In 2016, Chamblin was found. He was dating Laura Buckingham who was well known, having appeared on the cover of *Southern Indiana Living* with her son. It was a son of whom she wanted sole custody from her previous relationship with Brad Sutherland. The best way to be assured of having sole custody was to have Sutherland dead. Knowing that Chamblin was a former Marine sniper, she approached her new boyfriend to accomplish the task. At first Chamblin did not think she was serious, but her persistence in the matter convinced him otherwise. That is when he began to secretly tape their conversations. Chamblin then took the tapes to the police. With the cooperation of the police, Chamblin told Buckingham that he would not execute Sutherland but he would introduce her to someone who would. With her son frolicking in the back of the room, Buckingham paid an undercover police officer $3,000 to murder Sutherland. Buckingham was subsequently arrested. In Tennessee, Deputy Sheriff Tim Phillips applauds the Marine for preventing certain bloodshed. The Roane County sheriff said, "If she had gone to another source, they may have been able to complete this particular mission." *The Washington Post* reported that this story be consider as Chamblin's act of redemption.

To be lost, and then to be found; to live in sin, and then to be forgiven; to live in judgment, and then understand grace;

to be dead, and then to be alive; to be disobedient, and then to accept obedience — that is the message from our lesson today in Paul's letter to the churches in Rome. It is a story of redemption.

Our lesson today in Romans 5:12-19, is considered by biblical scholar William Barclay to be one of the most important passages in the New Testament. Barclay wrote that "no passage of the New Testament has had such an influence on theology as this." Barclay, who published a commentary series on the New Testament in 1955 which is still read today, and was a professor of biblical criticism at the University of Glasgow, should be taken seriously. The reason for Barclay's assessment is because in this passage we have the most succinct expression of Paul's understanding of salvation.

What Paul presents to us is a two-part story. If it were a play, we could consider it to be act one and act two.

Act one puts Adam on the stage before us and his disobedience. Adam was instructed by God that everything in the Garden of Eden was his to behold, except the fruit from the tree of the knowledge of good and evil. Enticed by Eve, Adam ate a piece of fruit from that tree. Tradition holds that is was an apple and it was with that act of disobedience that sin came into the world. It is a sin that you and I live in today. It is the sin of disobedience that you and I still practice today.

Act two puts Jesus on the stage before us and his obedience. It was because Jesus was perfectly obedient to God, and therefore without sin, that Jesus becomes our redeemer.

Paul considerered Adam and Jesus to be more than individuals, but corporate entities. In Adam, *all* of us have sinned. But in Christ, *all* of us can be saved. The decision is placed before us — will we live in disobedience or obedience? Will we leave the theater after act one, or will we stay after the intermission and live in act two?

Today is the first Sunday of Lent. Lent is to prepare us spiritually for Holy Week, that is, Good Friday and Easter.

Lent is therefore the season of the Christian Year for self-reflection. For the next forty days we are to reflect on whether we are living lives in disobedience or in obedience to God. We are to ask ourselves, am I living in Adam or am I living in Christ?

In the numerology of the Bible the number forty symbolizes the death of one's self and spiritual rebirth. Our purpose as we journey through Lent is spiritual rebirth. There are many important biblical references to the spiritual significance of forty days. All of these references refer to dying to one's self and the subsequent spiritual rebirth. We have before us the account that Moses spent forty days on Mount Sinai with God. We are told that Elijah spent forty days and nights walking to Mount Horeb. It is reported that God sent forty days and nights of rain in the great flood of Noah. It is recounted that the Hebrew people wandered forty years in the desert while traveling to the promised land. Jonah's prophecy of judgment gave forty days to the city of Nineveh in which to repent or be destroyed. Jesus retreated into the wilderness, where he fasted for forty days while being tempted by Satan. Tradition holds that the apostles fasted for forty hours while Jesus was in the tomb. The biblical reference to three days is understood to be spanning three days. But it would be forty hours from Friday afternoon to early Sunday morning.

Lent provides for us forty days of self-reflection. We have forty days to determine if we are living in disobedience or obedience. We have forty days to acknowledge that we are living a life in sin or that we are living a life in grace. We have forty days to decide if we are lost or if we have been found.

Augsburg, Germany, has embedded traffic lights in the pavement at intersections. This is because so many pedestrians are looking down at their hand-held phones that they are not looking at the oncoming traffic. A city spokeswoman said the embedded traffic lights "creates a whole new level of attention." The Chinese city of Chongqing made headlines when it experimented with a 165-foot of pavement where pedestrians had to choose between walking on a normal lane or one reserved for what they called "smombies." A smombie comes from combing the word smartphone with zombie to describe people who are staring at their smartphones rather than paying attention to their surroundings. In the United States it is reported that one in three people are busy texting or working on their smartphone at dangerous intersections.

I surmise that during Lent we are going have to decide if we are a smombie or spiritually awake. We are going to have to decide if we are going to be looking down or be looking up. We are going to have to decide if we are going to have a whole new level of attention. We are going to have to make a decision — which lane are we going to be walking in?

Let us once again take our seat in the theater.

It is act one and we are on stage with Adam in the Garden of Eden. Adam has just eaten the forbidden fruit. He tries to make an excuse for his transgression, saying that Eve coerced him into eating the apple. But, Adam knows he is responsible for what he has done. We always need to remember that in the middle of the word sin is the letter "I." We stand front and center in our sins. We must take responsibility for our transgressions.

We cannot justify what we have done by saying it was only a little white lie. Somehow sexual transgressions always seem to be at the top of the hierarchy of sin, and we ignore how devastating it is to be critical of others. Consumed by the evening news we conclude that we are not murders and that we have not engaged in financial shenanigans. So, we deceive ourselves into thinking that we are okay. But, let's take sin off the television screen for a moment and bring it down into the pew where we sit. How many people have we murdered with our gossip? How many people have we bankrupted with our nit-picking? Now, sin has become a bit more realistic and we can no longer blame Eve.

Jesus discussed the nature of sin and they all point to the same thing — our being self-righteous. It is the thinking that I can do no wrong. In false humility we say to others I am a sinner, but then we go on to judge and condemn anyone whom we don't agree with or whom we do not like. The pervasiveness of sin is found in our conceit: our stubbornness, our complaining, our criticisms, our judgments, and our "isms" — sexism, racism, ageism.

We do stand on the stage alone with Adam. Eve is not to be seen and everyone in the theater is watching us.

The New York Times tells the story of Vijay Mallya, of New Delhi, India, who called himself the "king of good times." And the multi-billionaire was. He made his fortune in the beer and airline industries. He hobnobbed with the rich and famous. He had several lavish homes and hosted magnificent parties. He was proud of the swimsuit calendar he published each year. Mallya was the king of good times because he used other people's money. When India faced financial ruin the banks lowered their requirements for receiving loans. Mallya used this opportunity to transform his Kingfisher Airlines from an economy transport to one of luxury. This resulted in bankruptcy, and the king of good times left India with 1.5 billion dollars in unpaid bills.

Yes, we are the king of good times. We are the king and queen of self-centeredness. We must recognize and confess that we are disobedient. Otherwise there is no need for us to walk in the Lenten lane toward Holy Week.

The intermission is over and we have returned to our seats. We do not like this life of sin, so we wonder if the next act in the drama of life has an answer for us. The houselights have been dimmed. This is synonymous with the shadow of sin that engulfs us.

It is now act two and we stand on the stage with Jesus. The prop behind us is a rolled away stone and an empty tomb. We know that Jesus through his death and resurrection is the redeemer of humanity.

If we have journeyed successfully through Lent we are able to believe this — that the tomb is indeed empty. We know that our sins are now forgiven and that we have eternal life. We know that we no longer live under condemnation, but that we now live by grace. We know this because Lent has prepared us to accept this by faith.

But, there is a requirement for a successful journey through Lent. It is called obedience. It means that during the next forty days we no longer look down, but that we look up. It means that we are no longer self-centered but others centered. Or, as Rick Warren, the mega-church pastor of Saddleback Church in Lake Forest, California, who wrote in the opening line of his hugely popular book *The Purpose-Driven Life*, "It's not about you." This statement has become a common mantra for Christians. "It's not about you."

It is not about me, because it is about God and others. That is the understanding that must come upon us on our spiritual walk to Calvary.

If we are to be obedient then we must engage in the spiritual disciplines that will enforce that obedience. This morning we have already accomplished the most basic, and that is attending worship. We should enhance this experience by being involved in the church's Sunday school program. We must go one step further and find a ministry and mission project of the church to be engaged in. And let us not diminish the importance of being a part of a small group sponsored by the church.

Beyond these corporate experiences there is our individual pilgrimage. We must read the Bible and pray daily. We must read devotional literature, and we must always ask ourselves if our behavior is one of disobedience or obedience.

This is Paul's understanding that though we have sinned through Adam, we are saved through Christ.

John Knox's name is synonymous with the Scottish Reformation of the mid-1500s. Knox was an outspoken critic of the Catholicism that ruled the country and prevented the Lutheran expression of the Protestant Reformation. Knox was so outspoken in his advocacy of reform that he was called the "Thundering Scot." Having angered Mary Queen of Scots he was arrested and sentenced to serve in the galleys. The galley is where those sentenced sat in the hold of a ship and were forced to row. In a dark hour his ship passed within the sound of the bells of Saint Andrews Cathedral, and Knox resolved, "I shall yet live to preach there." Knox was able to escape his imprisonment and relocated to Geneva. When the Queen's daughter Mary of Guise was on the throne, Knox returned to Scotland. But Knox was still as resolute as before. Without compromise Knox said to the newly appointed ruler, "I am sent to preach the evangel of Jesus Christ to such as please to hear it; and it has two parts, repentance and faith."

The season of Lent has two parts — repentance and faith.

To Cross Over

British writer Philip Norman completed his third book on the Beatles. This 800 page volume was a biography of Paul McCartney. Before researching the biography Norman thought that McCartney with all his musical talent must be very pleased with himself, only to discover that the opposite was true. Norman said he came to realize that the living rock legend, and I quote, is "also insecure... he's in his seventies now, and he still thinks he has to prove himself virtually every night onstage." Norman went on to say that McCartney's security comes from the adulation of his audience. McCartney's need for the affirmation of an audience is summed up by Norman with this observation, "The love that comes to Paul is so immense, from so many people, he can't do without it, really."

Insecure. That could probably describe most of us, if not all of us. We question. We doubt. We wonder. We worry. Perhaps at the top of the list is the insecurity of money. But, there are many other things to ponder: health, family, friends, work, and all of this leaves us in a quandary of insecurity.

How do we overcome that insecurity? We seek the adoration of adoring fans who pay an exorbitant amount of money to purchase a ticket to come and see us perform. Those flashing light bulbs, the waving arms, the selfies, must mean that we are okay — that we are accepted, that we are worthy. But, we realize that that is not enough, so we have to get back up on that stage the next night. And the next night. And the next night.

So we seek a way to combat our insecurity. If I only had more money. If I only had more friends. If I only could have gotten that promotion. If I could only live in that new house. If I only could buy that new car. If I only could...If I only could... If I only could... and the list is endless. But we know that with that next raise will only come with it a search for something more.

I have a friend* who was a chaplain in the Army. He shared how sad it was to see someone get promoted. As a lieutenant the only thing they wanted was to become a captain. But several days after they became a captain, all they wanted to do was become a major. They were dissatisfied and insecure, only days after they were promoted — only days after they reached their goal. Then came the worry and the insecurity of making the next promotion and in their quest to be promoted, in their quest to overcome insecurity, they made life miserable for their subordinates.

We live in an insecure environment. There are many things we cannot control, and a few things that we can. But they all leave us in fear — in a panic.

There are the things that we cannot control. Will the Zika virus come to my neighborhood? Will I be laid off? Will my illness be healed?

Then there is the insecurity of indecision. Did I buy the right appliance for my home? Did I choose the right physician? Did I make the right financial investment? Did I discipline my child properly? Did I say something wrong at the party?

All of this leaves us in a quandary of insecurity.

This then brings us to our lesson in our scripture reading for this morning. Paul shares with us in his letter to the churches in Rome the security that comes with faith. It is a faith that comes in trusting God. It is a faith that comes from knowing that God loves us and accepts us. It is a faith that comes from knowing that God will guide us. It is a faith that comes from knowing that God is the Creator and ruler of the universe. It is a faith that comes from knowing that nothing can separate us from the love of God.

This we can come to accept with confidence for we can believe what Paul later wrote with such elegance in Romans: "Who shall separate us from the love of Christ? Shall trouble or hardship or persecution or famine or nakedness or danger or sword? No, in all these things we are more than conquerors through him who loved us. For I am convinced that neither death nor life, neither angels nor demons, neither the present nor the future, nor any powers, neither heighth nor depth, nor anything else in all creation, will be able to separate us from the love of God that is in Christ Jesus our Lord."

This is the faith that conquers insecurity. It is trusting in the overpowering omnipresence and omnipotence of God.

"Jesus Loves Me" remains the most popular children's hymn. It is also the most notable hymn that missionaries use to teach children the message of Jesus. The hymn was originally written as a poem in 1860 by Anna Bartlett Warner. Her sister, Susan, was a novelist. Behind Harriet Beecher Stowe's novel *Uncle Tom's Cabin*, Susan's novel, *The Wide, Wide World* was ranked second in popularity. The hymn comes from another novel that Susan wrote at the time titled *Say and Seal*. Today few are aware of that novel, but everyone is familiar with the poem that Anna wrote for one of the characters in Susan's novel. In the novel as Mr. Linden comforts the dying child Johnny Fax he recites the poem, "Jesus loves me! this I know, for the Bible tells me so." In 1861, Dr. William B. Bradbury put the poem to music. It first appeared in 1862 in his hymnal *The Golden Shower*. The hymn has remained unchanged to this day.

Jesus loves me, this I know, for the Bible tells me so. It is this love of Jesus that allows us to overcome our insecurities and live in hope. It is our faith in the love and presence of Jesus that provides our security in an unknown future.

"Jesus loves me, this I know, for the Bible tells me so." What does the Bible say about love and hope? It comes, according to Paul, with faith.

Faith is a difficult concept to understand. The writer of Hebrews gave us a good definition: "Faith is the substance of things hoped for, the evidence of things not seen." Perhaps even a better definition comes from Archie Bunker, that chauvinist who was the head of the household on the television series *All in the Family*, as Archie once said, "Faith is something you believe that nobody in his right mind would believe."

Faith is a difficult concept to understand. Faith is a difficult concept to grasp. Certainly faith is a concept that is difficult to articulate. This is why Paul began his lesson by giving us an example of faith as demonstrated in the life of Abraham. By referring to Abraham, Paul wanted to give us a concrete example of faith that we could understand, grasp, and articulate. If we can understand the faith of Abraham we will better be able to understand what it means to have faith in God. Paul also wanted to show, by using Abraham, that faith always precedes action.

Paul did not arbitrarily select Abraham as his example of faith, but he had some well calculated reasons for doing so. Abraham is considered to be one of the forefathers of Judaism. By discussing the faith of Abraham Paul would have the ear of his Jewish audience. Jesus came from the lineage of Abraham, which means Paul would have the ear of his Christian constituents. But most importantly for both congregations is that Abraham's faith preceded his actions. Faith came before the law of Judaism. Faith came before Christian discipleship. Faith, for both groups, came before works. Our actions show our faith, but faith must come first. We must believe before we can act. This is Paul's underlying message. Before there is anything else in our religious experience, we must first have faith.

We must live a life that is a doxology. We must first praise God from whom all blessings come before we can follow God in steadfast service.

For Paul, Abraham's life was a doxology of faith. For Paul, Abraham' life was a life of faith.

Abraham was living peacefully in the valley of Ur, which was located between the Tigris and Euphrates rivers in Mesopotamia. This is also known as the Fertile Crescent because of its abundance. The Fertile Crescent is in present day Iraq. Abraham heard the call of God to take his family and tribesmen out of the land of the Chaldeans to the land of Canaan, which is today Israel. Abraham was to take his people to the promised land. This took place approximately 1,900 years before Christ, or about 4,000 years ago. Abraham on faith answered that call.

The people who accompanied Abraham were called Hebrews, which means "to cross over," because they had the faith to cross over the Euphrates River and follow the promise of God.

What is most important in this story for Paul, and subsequently for us, is that Abraham had faith in the command of God before he acted. Faith comes before actions. What is significant with this act of faith is Abraham established the belief in one God as the supreme ruler of the universe.

This is called monotheism. Up to this point all religions were polytheistic meaning they believed in many gods, each controlling one aspect of creation. Abraham in his faith established monotheism, the belief in only one supreme being. There are only three monotheistic religions — Judaism, Christianity, and Islam — and all three trace their origins to the faith of Abraham.

According to the scriptures Abraham was 75 years old when he received his calling from God. His name at the time was Abram, which means "God is exalted." Abram's name was later changed to Abraham which means "the father of many nations." Thus, Abraham is the father of Judaism, Christianity, and Islam.

From the story of Abraham we learn that before we can be engaged in any kind of service we must first believe in the power and presence of God. Before we can embark on any ministry or mission for the church we must first be empowered by our belief in God.

We also learn from Abraham that it is our faith in God that will sustain us during our difficult times. It is our faith in God that will give us hope in the midst of life's tragedies. It is our faith in God that will calm our doubts. It is our faith in God that will give us security when we are plagued by insecurity.

We must believe before we can act. We must believe before we can cross over.

The idea for the Christian flag emerged on Sunday, September 26, 1897, when a speaker failed to show up for a rally at Brighton Chapel on Coney Island, the recreational area for New York City. Sunday school superintendent Charles Overton thought quickly on how to fill the void. He decided to turn the American flag into an object lesson. Using the colors of the American flag, Overton said the Christian flag should have white for purity, innocence, and peace. The flag's blue panel should symbolize faith, trust, and sincerity. The flag would have a red cross to remind us of our Savior's sacrifice.

Whenever we look to the Christian flag in our sanctuary we should see an emblem of faith. Whenever we look to the characters in the Bible we should see testimonials to faith. Whenever we see others seated in the sanctuary among us we should see living examples of faith. This becomes our inspiration to have faith, to believe, to trust, to be secure when confronted daily be our insecurities.

As it is written in Hebrews, "Therefore, since we are surrounded by such a great cloud of witnesses, let us throw off everything that hinders and the sin that so easily entangles. And let us run with perseverance the race marked out for us." We are not talking about the Microsoft® cloud, but a cloud that we can see and embrace. It is the cloud of witnesses that through the centuries, through millenniums to be exact, that have followed Abraham across the Euphrates into the promised land. These individuals have supported us and strengthened our faith. You and I can only pray that we can be a part of that same cloud of witnesses for others.

Rowland Hill was a pastor in the Church of England in the early 1800s. Hill was known to be untroubled at offending others in his sermons. It is reported that he was once preaching to a group of farmers and compared them to their pigs. He preached that as a pig never looks up at the oak tree from which the acorn is dropped that feeds them, just as the farmers never looked up to God who provided their blessings. Though Hill was educated at some of the best schools in England, because he was so outspoken churches would not let him use their pulpits, so he began to preach outdoors in the fields. Because of Hill's outspoken style, he was a successful evangelist. Rowland Hill's last words before his death on Thursday, April 11, 1833, were these, "I have no rapturous joys, but peace — good hope, through grace, all through grace."

Grace, hope, security — they are the hallmarks of a life lived in faith.

Invictus

Luther Haden Taylor was born on February 21, 1875, in Oskaloosa, Kansas. Taylor is a legend in baseball having played with the New York Giants before the franchise moved to San Francisco. He played with the team for nine years, from 1900 to 1908, while the team was still at the Polo Grounds in Upper Manhattan. As a pitcher, he helped the Giants win their first World Series of the modern baseball era in 1905. For his career Taylor was 115-103, with a 2.77 earned run average. Taylor was devastating on the mound because of his unorthodox corkscrew delivery. His best pitch was a destructive drop ball.

Luther Haden Taylor was known by his teammates and the public as Dummy Taylor, because he was a deaf and mute. Taylor could not hear and he could not speak. In the early 1900s deaf and mute individuals were routinely called dumb, and this great baseball player was no exception.

Growing up Taylor attended the Kansas School for the Deaf where he was an outstanding athlete and the class valedictorian. When Taylor ended his playing career, he was an umpire. When that chapter of his life was closed, he returned to the Kansas School for the Deaf where he coached the baseball team. Taylor contributes his long life of 82 years to his physical fitness regime, which centered on boxing as exercise.

The Giant's players learned to sign so they could converse with Taylor. For a very short time Taylor played for Cleveland, but since the players refused to learn how to sign he returned to the Giants. When Taylor was scheduled to pitch the stands were full of fans that like him could not hear or speak. Those fans became known as Taylor's "silent fraternity."

It should be known that Taylor was the only deaf and mute player to ever be thrown out of a game by an umpire. Unimpressed with an umpire's calls, Taylor walked over to the official, stuck out his chin, and mouthed words that could not be misinterpreted.

But what is important about Taylor's life is how he overcame his handicap. He is credited with perfecting signing between the pitcher and the catcher, so the man behind the plate could communicate with the man on the mound. As we see catchers signing to pitchers today, it goes back to 1900 and Dummy Taylor. But Taylor was not dumb. When he was confronted by an obstacle, he creatively persevered and overcame it.

That is the lesson from our reading in Romans this morning. It is about overcoming hardships, difficulties, and obstacles. It is about overcoming worries, pain, and suffering. It is about overcoming disappointments, disillusionments, and disenchantments.

The solution that Paul offers us is one that we have heard so often. Paul wrote, "We know that suffering produces endurance, and endurance produces character, and character produces hope, and hope does not disappoint us." But, as the old saying goes, "It is easier said than done."

Perhaps it *is* easier to recite Paul's words than it is to live them. But, living them will become easier if we understand Paul's intentions when he penned these phrases. Perhaps we also confuse what Paul wrote as being rather glib. But, what Paul discussed is obtainable if we understand the meaning behind the phrases. Perhaps we also dismiss what Paul wrote as being naïve. But, what Paul wrote is very practical for those who have faith. Perhaps we think that Paul's solution is only for the super religious. But, what Paul wrote can sustain the most disinherited.

We begin with suffering. We are all so familiar with suffering that we probably do not even have to discuss that point in this sermon. But, it would be good for us to know that Paul was familiar with suffering. Paul's daily encounter with suffering gives credence to his solution. In Paul's letter to the church in Corinth he offered a summary of the sufferings he endured in life. This rendition of hardships is related to Paul being a missionary. But, is the suffering of a missionary any different from that of a housewife, a business person, a student, someone who is ill, or someone who has family problems? Suffering is suffering no matter how the cloud covers us.

Paul outlined his agonies with these words: "I have worked in prison more frequently, been flogged more severely, and been exposed to death again and again. Five times I received from the Jews the forty lashes minus one. Three times I was beaten with rods, and once I was pelted with stones. Three times I was shipwrecked, I spent a night and a day in the open sea. I have been in danger from rivers, in danger from bandits, in danger from my fellow Jews, in danger from Gentiles; in danger in the city, in danger in the country, in danger at sea; and in danger from false believers. I have labored, toiled, and have often gone without sleep; I have known hunger and thirst and have often gone without food; I have been cold and naked. Besides everything else, I faced daily the pressure of my concern for all the churches."

Somewhere in that list you and I should find ourselves. Prison — perhaps we are imprisoned by our sins. Flogged — perhaps the gossip of another person has cut us. Beaten — perhaps we have been bruised by criticism. Shipwrecked — perhaps despair has left us floundering. Bandits — perhaps illness has robbed us. False believers — perhaps we are disquieted by a secular society. Hungry — perhaps the lack of money is a serious issue. Somewhere in that list, probably in several places in that list, you and I will find ourselves.

On Tuesday, July 31, 2012, at 1:05 p.m., the northern electrical grid in India collapsed. This happened when the country was trying to develop itself into the would-be Asian power source. Shortly after that, two more grids collapsed and twenty million people were in a blackout. The blackout covered twenty of India's 28 states, stretching from the border with Myanmar in the northeast to the Pakistan border about 1,800 miles away. It was the largest blackout in the history of the world.

Could it be that our sufferings and hardships make it seem like we are living in the largest blackout in the history of the world. And let us be honest, if it is my problem, it is the biggest problem. We can always find someone who is seemingly worse off, but that does not diminish the size of my suffering. It is real, because it is me.

Suffering produces endurance, character, and hope. In order for us to realize that Paul is not being flippant, that he is not being simplistic, we must first look at the meaning of the word grace, in which he began this passage.

Paul wrote that through "Jesus we obtained access to grace." The Greek word that Paul uses for grace is *prosagoge*. It is a word that means to be safe, to be secure, to be protected, to be at peace. In the Greek it has two different but similar applications, both of which Paul incorporated into his letter. It is the word that describes ushering someone into the presence of royalty. Grace, for Paul, would then mean bringing us into the presence of the King of kings, Jesus the Christ. In the Greek the word also means a ship coming into a harbor. The ship having been tossed about in the open sea now finds calm water in the safety of the harbor. For Paul then the word grace means to be sheltered from life's problems. Paul used the word grace in his letter to mean we are safe, we are secure, we are protected, we are at peace, by something bigger, by something more important, by something more powerful, than ourselves.

For Paul knowing that we are in the presence of the King of kings, that we are in a safe and protected harbor, allows us to endure our suffering and hardships. Endurance can also mean perseverance. This does not mean our problems are not real. This does not mean that our problems are not serious. But it does mean that by having faith in the King of kings we shall endure. We shall persevere. We shall endure, we shall persevere, because of our faith in our heavenly parent who is the creator and sustainer of the universe.

Endurance produces character.

We often hear about it being okay to have a little less character if it meant a little less suffering.

What we need to do is put the word character into the perspective on how Paul used it in his letter. Paul is writing to the Christians in Rome, and it is difficult to be a Christian in Rome as the church is persecuted. Earlier in this sermon we read Paul's list of sufferings he endured as a missionary. These are the same sufferings that the persecuted Christians in Rome were enduring. And this suffering produces character.

The Greek word that Paul uses for character is *dokime*. It is used for metal that has passed through the fire and the impurities have been purged out of it. For Paul this meant what he had endured as a missionary and what the Christians in Rome were enduring through their persecution, would purify their faith. It would make them stronger in their faith. We should never think that suffering is good, but suffering can make us more aware of our faith, and strengthen our need for faith.

The name of Helen Keller is familiar to most of us. She was born on June 27, 1880, in West Tuscumbia, Alabama. When she was nineteen months old she became ill with either scarlet fever or meningitis, we don't know which, that left her deaf and blind. At the age of six Helen was taught to communicate by Anne Sullivan. The first word that Anne signed into Hellen's palm was the word "doll." In her adult years, Keller went on to become a political activist and lecturer. Helen Keller, who understood suffering, but also understood endurance and character, once said, "Although the world is full of suffering, it is also full of the overcoming of it."

The ability to overcome suffering results in endurance and character .

William Ernest Henley was a poet. He had tuberculosis which caused him to have his left leg amputated below the knee. Lying in bed at the Edinburgh Infirmary, Henley faced the prospect of having his right leg amputated. This suffering, this fear, inspired Henley in 1875 to write the poem *Invictus*, a poem of endurance and character. It begins with these words:

> *Out of the night that covers me,*
> *Black as the pit from pole to pole,*
> *I thank whatever gods may be*
> *For my unconquerable soul.***

"For my unconquerable soul." So inspiring was Henley, that his good friend Robert Louis Stevenson based his one-legged character Long John Silver on Henley. And today you may have heard of the *Invictus* games, which are sporting events played by disabled veterans. In Latin the word invictus means unconquerable.

For Paul, if we have faith in the King of kings our souls cannot be conquered.

Paul wrote that it is by grace that we have endurance and character in the midst of our suffering. But we also have something that is even more important than these, and that is hope. Paul wrote that the assurance of God's love gives us hope. Paul wrote that the outpouring of the Holy Spirit gives us hope. We have hope in our future, no matter how tragic our suffering is today, because of the assurance of God's love and because God has filled us with his presence we always have hope in our future.

The discussion of hope is an eschatological discussion by Paul. Eschatology comes from the Greek word *eschatos* which means last or farthest, and the suffix *logy* means study. Eschatology is the branch of theology that deals with the end times. Paul's message of hope is that as painful as suffering is today, eschatologically speaking, it will not be with us forever. Our soul shall remain unconquered by suffering.

Paul Hubbard was six years older than Luther Taylor, but both boys attended the Kansas School for the Deaf and both boys were active in sports — Taylor in baseball, Hubbard in football. Hubbard went on to be the quarterback at Gallaudet College, a college for the deaf in Washington DC. Today Gallaudet is a university. Hubbard made several innovations to the game of football while he was at Gallaudet. Gallaudet College created an innovation for football by having large drums placed on the sidelines so players would be aware of the snap count through the vibrations in their feet. This is no longer a part of football, but another Hubbard innovation is. Hubbard created the football huddle so opposing players would not see him signing the next play. The football huddle is very much a part of the game today. Hubbard experienced suffering. Hubbard was able to endure. Hubbard developed character. Hubbard had hope.

Invictus — unconquerable.

**If you have a screen in your sanctuary you may want to project this poem on it.

Ephesians 5:8-14
Lent 4

Bible Wagon

"Sleeper, awake! Rise from the dead, and Christ will shine on you." Paul concluded this section of his lesson to the church in Emphasis, which was our reading this morning, with a quote from a hymn. As it is with us today, the hymn stanza would be instantly recognizable along with the message that was associated with the hymn. If anyone in the congregation was uncertain of the message that Paul was trying to convey, there would be immediate clarification when they heard the words of a very familiar hymn. It is the message that the light of Christ will overcome the darkness of evil.

"Sleeper, awake! Rise from the dead, and Christ will shine on you." This stanza came from a very important and well-known hymn to the first-century Christians because it was probably sung as a part of their baptismal liturgy. We are not certain it was a part of the baptismal liturgy, but its message and format make baptism its most probable use. As the adult who was baptized, who was fully immersed in the water, as he or she came up out of the water the congregation standing on the shore would sing "Sleeper, awake! Rise from the dead, and Christ will shine on you." The baptized individual has now awakened from darkness into the light of Christ. The baptized individual is no longer asleep in sin but alive in Christ.

The earliest complete account of the baptismal liturgy of the church comes to us in the year 200 AD by Hippolytus as he recorded it in his book *The Apostolic Tradition*. *Hippolytus*, who resided in Rome, is considered to be the most important third-century theologian in the church. Because of the place that Hippolytus held in the church and because of the title of his book, it is believed that the liturgical practices that he recorded date back to the first years of the church, and most certainly to the time of Paul.

From the writings of Hippolytus we know the early church's practice regarding baptism. Those desiring to be baptized were brought before the leaders of the church. Certain individuals were automatically disqualified for consideration. These would be: prostitutes, pimps, actors, circus performers, soldiers, gladiators, and certain government officials. Those selected to be considered for baptism studied for three years under careful supervision. This long period of preparation was called the catechumenate from which we get our word catechism, which means apostle's instruction. Attendance at worship was also required during these years. During these years the candidates would study, pray, fast, and were taught the Apostles' Creed and the Lord's Prayer. There would also be continued rites of exorcism intended to release the catechumen from the power of the devil. At the end of three years the congregation had to vote on each penitent's acceptance.

The liturgical rite of baptism began before dawn on Easter Day, the only day of the year that baptisms were performed. During the night a prayer vigil was held with scripture reading. At sunlight the candidates came to the water's edge barefoot and wearing rough clothing made of animal hair. This symbolized their life in sin. They were then stripped naked, with men and women discretely separated to protect their privacy. Three times the oil of exorcism was placed on them. Each time the candidate would face west, in the direction of the setting sun and darkness. Then the candidate would face east, in the direction of the rising sun and light. The candidate would then be asked three questions, answering each with the words "I believe." The first question: "Do you believe in God the Father almighty?" The second question: "Do you believe in Christ Jesus, the Son of God…" and this question would continue with a portion of the Apostle's Creed as we know it today. The third question, "Do you believe in the Holy Spirit…" and again the question would continue with a portion of the Apostle's Creed as we know it today.

The candidate would then be immersed. As the candidate came up out of the water the congregation would sing a baptismal hymn, while the newly inducted Christian was given shoes, a white robe to wear, and a lighted candle. Then the bishop would lay his hands upon them and with oil make the sign of the cross on their foreheads. All the worshipers would then celebrate the Lord's Supper.

"Sleeper, awake! Rise from the dead, and Christ will shine on you."

The baptismal liturgy is a symbolic representation that Christians are to be the light of the world that overcomes the darkness of evil. They are to be the shoes of discipleship, the white robe of martyrdom, and the candle to give light to a dark world. It is the message that Paul wrote about in our reading this morning and why he selected a baptismal hymn to emphasize his message of Christians being the light that will expose the darkness of evil.

We live in a dark world. The darkness that Paul speaks of in this passage is not the darkness that comes from ill health or disappointment, but the darkness that comes from corruption, greed, selfishness, and dishonesty. Paul wrote that we are to expose, and I quote, the "unfruitful works of darkness."

Preachers often like to be melodramatic by saying we now live in the worse time in the history of the world, which is not accurate for every decade has been engulfed by dark shadows. You don't need to look any further back than the Holocaust to know that. But, this does not negate the fact that a dark foreboding storm cloud shadows our land today. ISIS should be the only answer we need for that.

43

Yet, ISIS is rather distant from the darkness that engulfs our own lives and permeates our communities. In fact, sometimes the light shines dimly in our own church planted next to the curb on Main Street USA.

In order to understand the evil that Paul is concerned about we need to place our scripture reading this morning in the total context of Paul's letter to the church in Ephesus. Paul wrote of eight evils and eight virtues in his letter. Our lesson for this morning is the sixth one in that list. He presented his list in the form of an antithesis. As I read the list you will understand darkness in the world versus the light in the world.

The first is falsehood versus truth.

Second is resentment versus self-control.

Third is stealing versus generosity.

Fourth is evil speech versus edification.

Fifth is malice versus love

Sixth, which is our lesson, is impurity versus purity.

Seventh is imprudence versus wisdom.

Eighth is debauchery versus joy.

The darkness of the world that is to be exposed is falsehood, resentment, stealing, evil speech, malice, impurity, imprudence, and debauchery. We have all experienced the fog created by unsavory behavior. We have all experienced the bleakness that accompanies people who are self-centered. We have all experienced gloom when we encounter corruption. This was a part of the society that surrounded the church in Ephesus, as it surrounds us here in this time and in this place.

It is this unfruitful work of darkness that we are to expose with the light of Christ. The light is truth, self-control, generosity, edification of others, love, purity, wisdom, and joy. As we are a part of a church family, the Body of Christ, we know the blessings of being surrounded by children of the light. Those of us sitting in the pews of this sanctuary are good people, maybe not perfect, but good people nonetheless, who are a blessing to others and this community.

Paul wrote you "are" the light. That needs to be repeated. You are, the word is are, you are the light of the world. You and I, baptized Christians, are the light that shines in a dark and foreboding world.

Richie Incognito has a reputation as permanent as the myriad of tattoos on his muscular frame. He also has the reputation of being the NFL's most notorious bully. As a player for the Miami Dolphins he forced another player to leave the game because of his harassment. His threatening and racial text messages were too overbearing for the player on the receiving end of his diatribes. So severe was Incognito's misbehavior that his bullying became the defining moment for a team that had a dismal 2013 season of .500, going 8-8.

It is so sad and disheartening that bullies seem to rule. They use the power of their position, their money, and their status, to get their own way and make life miserable for everyone else. They can be stubborn and uncompromising as they trample on the defenseless. They have a scorched earth approach to life as long as it is not their garden that burns.

We are the light in a world of bullies. We are to expose bullies with love and generosity. We are to counteract their misdeeds with our deeds of justice and compassion. Paul wrote in our lesson, and I quote, "the fruit of our light is found in all that is good and right and true" — good, right, and true.

Ukrainian singer Jamala won the 2016 Eurovision Song Contest with her song "1944." It was a song about Soviet dictator Josef Stalin's deportation of the Crimean Tatars, a Turkic ethnic group that lived on the Crimean Peninsula. Stalin deported the Crimean Tatars fearful that he could not politically control them during Russia's war with Nazi Germany. Many died during the deportation. Many of those who did survive the arduous trip starved to death on the barren steppes of central Asia where they were relocated. This was a dark day in the history of Soviet Union. Jamal is a stage name. Jamal's real name is Susana Jamaladinova. The 32-year-old is a trained opera singer whose great-grandmother was deported in 1944. Nearly 20 million people globally watched her perform at Eurovision. In selecting the song "1944" Jamala said, "I was sure that if you sing, if you talk about the truth, it really can touch people."

We are to touch a person with that which is good, right, and true. A candle may be a small light, but it does burn bright in a darkened room. And a sanctuary full of candles can illuminate an entire community.

On April 29, 1854, missionary James Calvert was ecstatic as he heard the death drums beating. After years of evangelizing and teaching the gospel the Fijiian chief on Viwa Island ordered that the death drums that once were used to announce a human sacrifice, were now calling everyone to come and worship in the mission chapel. The darkness of human sacrifice was now conquered by the light of the gospel message.

We can make a loving difference in the world. We can make a loving difference in the lives of our family members, our friends, and our coworkers. We can make a loving difference in the life of the parishioner sitting beside you and in the pew across the aisle from you. We can make a loving difference in the life of a stranger. We can make a loving difference in the life of someone who has only known darkness.

The American Bible Society opened its doors on May 11, 1816. The first president was Elias Boudinot, who was also the first president of the Continental Congress. The second president was John Jay, who was the first chief justice of the United States Supreme Court. The purpose of the American Bible Society was to distribute Bibles, especially in the time of crisis. During the Mexican War of the 1840s the ABS provided Mexican civilians with Bibles. During the American Civil War of the 1860s, the ABS had what was called a

"Bible wagon." The Bible wagon would drive through the middle of a battlefield distributing Bibles to soldiers both North and South. Today in Afghanistan the American Bible Society distributes camouflaged Bibles to our soldiers.

"Sleeper, awake! Rise from the dead, and Christ will shine on you."

Moksha

Evagrius Ponticus, also known as Evagrius the Solitary, was a Christian monk and ascetic who resided in a monastery in the Egyptian desert. Concerned with the temptations that besought people, in the year 375 AD he compiled a list of the eight terrible thoughts, also referred to as the eight evil temptations. The eight patterns of evil that Evanrius listed are: gluttony, greed, sloth, sorrow, lust, anger, vainglory, and pride. The list was not to be one of condemnation; rather, it was to raise awareness to our most compelling temptations so that we would be self-disciplined enough to avert our attention from them. Almost two centuries later, in the year 590, Pope Gregory I, also known as Pope Gregory the Great, revisited the list and refined it to seven by combining two and adding two more of his own. Gregory's list is more commonly known as the Seven Deadly Sins, which are: pride, envy, anger, sloth, greed, gluttony, and lust.

Now, some 1,400 years later, as we move into the twenty-first century, perhaps we ought to restore the list to eight. This time adding a temptation that had not appeared in the sixth century but is appropriate for a technological society of the 2000s. The new eighth temptation would be "fame." In *The New York Times* an article was printed on November 11, 2009, by Alessandra Stanley, who wrote, "Fame has a spellbinding power in American society, the one thing that can trump wealth, talent, breeding and even elected office. Reality shows and social Web sites like Facebook long ago knocked down barriers that kept ordinary people trapped in obscurity." For this reason Stanley wrote, "some people take huge risks for the freedom to be someone else — a celebrity." She lifted up as examples the Salahis' who crashed a White House state dinner, the Heene's who pretended a child was trapped in a runaway balloon, and the Gosselin's who showcased their eight children, all desiring to share the limelight of a reality television show.

May we pray that we are not lead into the temptation of seeking celebrity status as our lasting "fame," the false kingdom to which we choose to affiliate. Seeking notoriety as our dwelling place may highlight us in the *National Enquirer*, possibly even placing us on the cover of *People* magazine, and we could even be permanently record on page B2, the society page, in our local newspaper. But wasn't this the kingdom Satan desired Jesus to preside over?

The recognition that Jesus sought was not to be found in the fleeting fame of celebrity stardom or in the limited tenure of public politics. Instead, Jesus desired to rule in the hearts of men and women through the ages, the authentic kingdom of God — free of publicity but abounding in celestial recognition. If one should ever question his or her worth, ask by what standard is it being measured? Is being important authenticated by having your name displayed on a marquee or a name recorded in the Book of Life? Realizing this, Jesus easily discounted the unworthiness of Satan's offer to rule over earthly kingdoms. In so doing, Jesus directed our ambitions to focus on ministering to the lives of those with whom we are in contact with on a daily basis.

Indeed, this may be a small kingdom, and a kingdom that will never make us the star of a reality TV show. So it is a choice to be flamboyant on the *Bachelorette, Real Housewives, Survivor, Dancing with the Stars*, a guest on *The View*, or to be a discreet member of the kingdom of God? To which do you aspire to be recognized by — Mark Burnett or Jesus?

However you count, be it six or seven or eight, sin is an act of disobedience to God. A sin is often measured as little or big, such as a "little white lie," which usually means a harmless lie; but is it possible for a sin to be harmless, measured on any scale? When we engage in the acts of pride, envy, anger, sloth, greed, gluttony, lust, and fame it demonstrates a disregard for God and a disdain for others.

I do not promote Hinduism, but it has an insightful understanding of living a life of passion versus a life of virtue.

The religion of Hinduism understands the entrapment of living a self-centered life. Hinduism is the oldest established religion in the world and the third largest. At the end of the first century CE, the Laws of Manu were established. These laws report the four basic goals that motivate humanity, thus they have also come to be called the "Four Ends of Human Life." A young man should transcend from a lower level to the next until he discovers the true meaning of life.

The journey begins with kama or pleasure. It is to discover purpose by gratifying the senses. At this stage Kama-sutra may be a familiar phrase to us having become a part of the English language lexicon. Kama-sutra is the often quoted text for its descriptions of sexual intimacy. It is here, at kama, as a hedonist, that one begins the journey of life.

Unfulfilled, the young man moves to artha, which means financial success or wealth. This is the first attempt to set some real goals, but it reflects a misplaced ambition. He continues to sense an inner disquiet because in addition to being successful he equally desires to be respected.

Therefore he strives for dharma, which is righteous living. As a viable contributor to the community he knows he is doing good for others, but yet, there still remains an emptiness.

His goal now becomes moksha, which means liberation or spiritual freedom, and it is here that the real purpose of life is realized. Moksha is attained by separating the body from the mind, which becomes the realization of our true identity.

Sin is not an abstract concept, as we all dwell behind the dark curtain of kama. Perhaps we see sin each evening on the news; but, the real sin that we must recognize and acknowledge is what the front door of our homes conceals from others. Sin is not absent from the temples of righteousness, as steeples cast a foreboding shadow upon the pretenders of virtue.

In the 1970s Karl Menninger wrote a book that was widely read, studied, and discussed. Menninger was a Harvard educated psychiatrist who established the Menninger Sanitarium in 1925 in Topeka. As a psychiatrist he believed that mental health is dependent upon physical, social, cultural, moral, and spiritual health. A significant aspect of spiritual health is to be unencumbered by the ramifications of sin. Therefore his book, penned by a medical doctor, was titled *Whatever Became of Sin?* The following paragraph is the one that is most often quoted:

"The very word 'sin,' which seems to have disappeared, was a proud word. It was once a strong word, an ominous and serious word. It described a central point in every civilized human being's life plan and life style. But the word went away. It has almost disappeared — the word, along with the notion. Why? Doesn't anyone sin anymore? Doesn't anyone believe in sin?"

Has the word sin gone out of your vocabulary, or is it just reserved for the other person? Has sin gone out of your life, but lives abundant in your neighbors? Has sin avoided your church pew, but inhabits the pen that which is behind, in front, and across the aisle? If sin is not to be found in your life, then where is it?

Paul in his letter to the churches of Rome presents an uncompromising position that Christians will either live a life of sin or a life of righteousness. He writes, and I quote, "those who are in the flesh cannot please God." Flesh here does not mean the human body, but sinful desires. In contrast to that Paul writes, and I quote, "but the mind set on the Spirit is life and peace."

The Greek word that Paul uses for a man who lives by the human desires does not emanate from actions, but from his underlying attitude. Paul uses the Greek word *phronema* to contrast a life lived in the flesh or one lived in the Spirit. Earlier in Paul's letter he makes the distinction between a life lived in the flesh or a life lived in the Spirit by using the Greek word *phronema* — which means "attitude." Your attitude will be the defining factor if you live a life in the flesh or in the Spirit. Then, of course, your decision will be seen in your actions. The question for Paul is this: Is your mind set on Satan or on Christ?

As I discussed earlier in this sermon, Jesus discounted the unworthiness of Satan's offer to rule over earthly kingdoms. Jesus' attitude was focused on the heavenly kingdom, and thus his actions rebuked the temptations of Satan. Satan tempted the basic human needs of Jesus by offering to turn stones into bread. Satan tempted the authority of Jesus by challenging him to jump off the pinnacle of the temple. Satan tempted the ego of Jesus by offering to rule the kingdoms of the world. In each case, as difficult as it was, Jesus refused to participate because of his attitude, his mind, was God-centered.

We must always remember that first and foremost the Bible is a book of theology. And Luke in his gospel makes a significant theological observation. At the beginning of the gospel story, after the three temptations of Jesus in the desert Luke records, "After the devil had tempted Jesus in every way, he left him to wait until a better time." Satan, unable to tempt Jesus into disobedience, into living by the flesh, into having a worldly attitude, does not reappear again until the end of the gospel story when he tempts Judas. Luke wrote, "Then Satan entered Judas." When Satan entered and tempted Judas, Judas succumbed to the power of the flesh. Judas had an attitude that he knew better than God, so Judas betrayed Jesus to the high priest, the supreme ruler of Judaism in Jerusalem.

Between these bookends of Satan's appearance we have the theological message of the reigning kingdom of God. Between these bookends of Satan's first appearance tempting Jesus and then his absence until he reappeared entering Judas, the kingdom of God reigned supreme. It was during this period, during this period of the public ministry of Jesus that Satan was powerless. Satan the man of the flesh had no power over Jesus the man of the Spirit.

Luke in his gospel is making it crystal clear that Judas is the great tempter, the great deceiver, the great adversary. Luke makes it clear Satan desires for us to live by the flesh, while Jesus desires for us to love by the Spirit. Luke makes it clear that Satan wants us to have a self-centered attitude, while Jesus wants us to have an other-oriented attitude. It is Luke's summons that as Christians we are to live between the bookends, with our Spirit overpowering and conquering the evil of Satan.

We are to be the bookends that does not submit to temptation. We are the bookends that does not allow Satan to enter us. The question is during this season of Lent, when we arrive in Jerusalem on Palm Sunday, will Satan have entered us? Will we be a part of the crowd that cries "crucify him!" or will be part of the remaining faithful eleven invigorated by the Spirit?

Luke was not isolated in his theological perspective, for what Luke confessed was a part of the theology of the first century church. This is why Paul, who wrote decades before Luke, could incorporate the same theological understanding in our lesson this morning. Paul wrote, and I quote, "But you are not in the flesh; you are in the Spirit, since the Spirit of God dwells in you." Paul realizes that we live between the bookends. With Pentecost we have been given the Spirit, and that Spirit will remain with us to the end of time. As Paul writes, "If the Spirit of him who raised Jesus from the dead dwells in you, he who raised Christ from the dead will give life to your mortal bodies." This periscope is Paul's assurance that believers will have eternal life.

The challenge then, as presented to us by Paul, is to be sure that we permit the Spirit to dwell within us. It is Paul's quest that we all live spiritual lives. It is Paul's mandate that we accept the disciples required to maintain a spiritual life. It is Paul's inquiry of what will be the orientation of our attitude — flesh or Spirit. And Paul is very forthright in declaring that if we allow Jesus to dwell within our souls, we will be spiritual individuals. As Paul writes, "since the Spirit of God dwells in you."

And it does take a proper attitude to be spiritual. It takes focus. It takes discipline. It takes desire. It means we engage in all the spiritual opportunities traditionally offered by the church. We engage in our own journey of personal prayer, Bible reading, and reading Christian literature. And we don't read Christian romance novels, but good challenging books by accredited theologians. And let us be sure that we realize that Rick Warren, Joel Olsteen, and Joyce Meyers are not accredited theologians, but simply populist writers. In our spiritual journey, we are to attend worship and Sunday school. We are to participate in a small group. We are to become active in a church ministry.

Reverend Edward Garbett was a pastor in the Church of England. He wrote a book of devotions titled *The Family Prayer Book, or Morning and Evening Prayers for Every Day in the Year* that was published in 1864. In his devotional book Garbett compiled spiritual sayings from more than 200 religious leaders from over the centuries and then reflected upon them. He arranged his meditations following the full cycle of the Christian year. On Week Fifteen, Thursday Evening, he opened with a quote from the famous sixteenth century Carmelite nun St Teresa of Avila when she wrote, "Prayer is the only channel through which God's great graces and favors may flow into the soul." Reflecting on this Garbett began his meditation with these words, "Gracious

Father, we earnestly implore the gift of the Spirit, that he may dwell in our hearts, and incline us to think and do such things as please thee. Take from us all ignorance and hardness of heart and enable us to receive with meekness thy Word."

Today, this fifth Sunday of Lent, as we journey to Easter, with one bookend on Ash Wednesday and the other on Passion Sunday, let this be our prayer: "Gracious Father, we earnestly implore the gift of the Spirit, that he may dwell in our hearts."

Philippians 2:5-11
Passion / Palm Sunday

The Ear of the Heart

Carol Klein, with schoolbooks under one arm and a sheet of music under the other, got off the express train from Brooklyn to Manhattan. The year was 1957 and the 15-year-old was determined to be a singing sensation. Wearing bobby socks, white sneakers, and a black skirt with a pink poodle embroidered on it, she opened the New York City telephone book. Starting with the "As" in the directory, she visited every music industry executive until she found one who would record her songs.

After being turned away by several recording studios, ABC-Paramount invited her to record four songs. Five decades later we know her as Carol King who has over twenty solo albums. At the age of 71, King was the first woman, on May 22, 2013, to receive Library of Congress's Gershwin Prize for Popular Song. The award is named after the music-writing team of George and Ira Gershwin.

Whenever King performs at a concert, a large number of baby boomers are in the audience. They were the ones who knew her best in the 1960s and '70s. Regarding the boomer audiences King said, "They have connected with me, and in connecting with me, they're really connecting with themselves and thinking of where they were when they first heard one of my songs."

The reason why we enjoy music so much is because of its connective quality. We connect to a message, a place, a person, or a memory. That connection continues to interpret and sustain life for us, as it gives us a sense of purpose and meaning. *The Britannica Encyclopedia* defines music as, "art concerned with combining vocal or instrumental sounds for beauty of form or emotional expression, usually according to cultural standards of rhythm, melody, and in most Western music, harmony." The important point is the phrase "emotional expression." Music often articulates that which we feel but are unable to put into grammatical sentences.

This morning we celebrate Palm Sunday. It is the sabbath day when we celebrate the joyful entry of Jesus into the city of Jerusalem through the east gate as he came down from the Mount of Olives.

Sitting in the pews before me is a worshiping congregation that spans the ages from toddlers to octogenarians. But, on this sabbath day every person of every generation has something in common — we share in the same Palm Sunday experience. As we participated in the opening processional this morning with the waving of the palms, our octogenarians have participated in that same processional ritual for eighty years. It is the day we wave palms, wear brightly colored clothes, and sing triumphal hymns. And those hymns give us "emotional expression."

The scripture passage that I have selected to read and preach on each Sunday comes from the Revised Common Lectionary. The lectionary follows the calendar of the Christian year, with an appropriate scripture reading for that particular liturgical day. The lectionary provides a scripture passage from the Old Testament, the Epistles, and the Gospel.

Prior to the established lectionary the scriptural passages for each Sunday were selected helter-skelter, with no rhyme nor reason to them. This ambivalent approach dates back to the Medieval church. The Roman Catholic church realized that this was a problem because the scripture readings were not being presented in a systematic fashion and the readings did not correspond to the liturgical calendar. At the Second Vatican Council in the 1960s the church remedied this problem with the publication in 1969 of the first lectionary that was called the *Ordo Lectionem Missae*, which means "Order of the Readings for Mass." It established a correct systematic and liturgical reading of scripture for each Sunday on a recurring in a three-year cycle. The Protestant denominations in 1983 published The Common Lectionary based on the Ordo Lectionem Missae. In 1992, the Common Lectionary was replaced by the updated Revised Common Lectionary, which we are still using today. The epistle reading from Philippians for today, Palm Sunday, comes from the Revised Common Lectionary.

The epistle reading for today is a hymn that was sung by the first-century Christians and was recorded by Paul in Philippians. It is appropriate that we read a hymn today in worship because it gives us emotional expression for our celebration of Palm Sunday. The hymn stanzas follow the life of Christ from his preexistence with God, his life on earth, and his final enthronement in our celestial heaven.

The hymn we have in Philippines is a Christology hymn. There are six Christological hymns recorded in the New Testament. The Christological hymn that you would be most familiar with is the Prologue to John's gospel. "In the beginning was the Word, and the Word was with God..." The prologue to John's gospel, the first fourteen verses, was a Christological hymn sung in worship by first-century Christians.

The term Christology comes from the Latin *Christo*, which means Christ, and *logy*, which means knowledge. Christology is the study of the meaning of Christ. Christology is the part of theology that is concerned with the nature and work of Jesus, including the Incarnation, the Resurrection, and his human and divine nature.

A Christological hymn is a "Hymn to Christ." The doctrine embodied in these hymns is the cosmological role of Christ. Cosmology studies the origin and structure of the universe. The hymns are outlined in stages beginning with the preexistence of Jesus, his earthly ministry as one in the flesh, circling back to his ascension and enthronement. It is within this context that that the first-century Christians sang a Christological hymn in worship. The hymn gave them emotional expression.

As we study and live the message of the Philippian hymn, we too will be given emotional expression to our feelings on this Palm Sunday.

The hymn in Philippians, like all Christological hymns, was sung by Christians years prior to Paul placing it in his letter to the church at Philippi. Philippi was a city in eastern Macedonia, established by Philip II in 356 BC and abandoned in the fourteenth century after the Ottoman conquest. Paul visited Philippi on his second missionary journey in the years of 49 to 51. It was the first congregation Paul established in Europe. After leaving Philippi, Paul later wrote this letter of instruction to the Christians in Philippi. There familiarity with the stanzas and meaning of this hymn would assist them in understanding and interpreting the content of Paul's letter, as our familiar hymns help us understand the Bible today.

The Philippians hymn has five phases. These five phases follow this outline:

First: Jesus was preexistent with God
Second: Jesus became incarnate as a man
Third: Jesus lived the incarnate life
Fourth: Jesus ascended back to God
Fifth: Jesus is exalted with God

The hymn moves from Jesus being sovereign over creation to being enslaved within creation. Jesus in the "form" of God was preexistent and equal with God. But Jesus would not "grasp" this as he voluntarily surrendered himself to being in the form of a man. Jesus exchanged the divine mode of existence for a "slave" mode of existence. The significance of this is that Jesus experienced life as we do each day. After voluntarily humbling himself, Jesus was resurrected and ascended to heaven where he was once again exalted over creation. Jesus was given a new name; he is called Lord for he is the ruler over all creation. Before this name even the heathen gods bow in submission.

Verse 11 of our hymn is often considered one of the most important scriptural passages in the New Testament. That line is not only a part of a Christological hymn, but it contains one of the earliest creeds of the church which is, "Jesus Christ is Lord." Today we often recite in worship the Apostles Creed and Nicene Creed, which are rather lengthy and esoteric. But the earliest creed of the church is simply four words in which the entire doctrine of the church is confessed — "Jesus Christ is Lord."

It is appropriate that we read and even sing, if we had the music, the Philippian hymn today. Today is Passion Sunday, the first Sunday of Holy week. In the days ahead we will celebrate Maundy Thursday, Good Friday, and Easter. In the weeks following we will celebrate the Ascension.

These weeks contain acts of loyalty and acts of betrayal. We will read of doubts and confessions. We will read of denials and proclamations. We will read of bewilderment and faith. We will read about miracles. We will read about teachings. We will read about preaching. We will read about missions. We will read of the Great Commandment and the Great Commission. We will read about who Jesus was, is, and is to be. And we have a Christological hymn that allows us to understand that and give it emotional expression.

We have a hymn that shares with us the life and meaning of Jesus.

Bobby McFerrin is best known to us for his iconic 1988 feel-good hit song "Don't Worry, Be Happy." Since then he has received ten Grammy Awards. McFerrin's love of music came from his childhood. Whenever he was sick his mother would give him two things, medicine for his illness and, in McFerrin's words, "she'd give me music for my spirit." He went on to say, "Music does have incredible power to rearrange your insides, rearrange your thoughts, and heal your body."

McFerrin is back in the news with the release of his album titled "Spirityouall." This reads as "spirit you all," which is Mcferrin's personal testament of faith. The album includes his adaptations of traditional African-American spirituals and devotional songs that he composed. McFerrin believes that music has a transcendent spiritual power saying, "It elicits so many emotions. Music has a way of communicating... that language does not. It can go past language."

Music has that wonderful quality that it does go beyond words. Feelings, which cannot be enunciated in rhetoric, are garnered in verse. Emotions, which escape expression in dialect, are captured in lyrics. Belief, that has an aura of unreality and mystery about it, becomes comprehensible and intelligible in a line of metrical writing.

Since music "can go past language," Paul elected to insert Christological hymns in his letters.

In the first-century church, singing a hymn celebrated involvement in the Christ event. This is why they are Christological hymns for we participate in the five phases of Jesus existence. Paul uses the hymn to move beyond just the comprehension of the Christ event, but to allow worship to become a call to action. We are to act in accordance with our sons of praise.

So then, how are we to apply the Philippian Christological hymn to our lives as we leave this sanctuary this morning? Beyond the waving of palms what are we to do?

The Philippian hymn for Palm Sunday was selected by the editors for placement in the Revised Common Lectionary as a testimony to the meaning of Holy Week. During this coming sacred week we are to enter into the five phases of the life of Christ. The hymn tells us we are to live an incarnate life, one that is filled with the indwelling of the Holy Spirit. Finding ourselves in the garden, challenged as to our loyalty, we do not deny the Lord. Sitting at the table of the Lord on Maundy Thursday we take on the commission to be

Jesus' body and blood in our communities. On Good Friday, as we stand beneath the cross, we don't mock but we confess Jesus' deity.

It means on Easter day, when we learn that the tomb is empty, beyond it seeming to be preposterous, we still believe. Standing on the sea shore, we confess three times that we love Jesus. Standing on the sea shore next to the morning fire, we commit ourselves to feeding Jesus' sheep.

The singing of hymns for the edification of Jesus and to affirm our call to discipleship has always been a part of our Protestant heritage. Martin Luther, who is the founding father of Protestantism in the sixteenth century, translated hymns from Hebrew and Greek into Latin, a language in which his congregants were familiar. Luther expected parishioners to learn to sing. Luther required all worshipers to attend singing practices during the week, so they would be prepared to sing with eloquence and exuberance during the sabbath worship.

Hymns are an expression of our faith. Hymns are a means of instruction. Hymns create a unity among believers.

Dolores Hart was as beautiful as she was talented, which attests to why she was such a prominent actress and singer in the 1950s and 60s. Ah! She gave Elvis Presley his first on-screen movie kiss. Both as an endearing movie star and Broadway theatrical sensation, she was known and beloved by all. Her name placed upon the marquee was a guaranteed ticket seller. Then bewilderment befell her fans. Even perhaps, for some, it was anger. Certainly, most of all, there was disbelief. Ms. Hart gave up a lucrative and promising show business career to become a Roman Catholic Benedictine nun. She no longer lived a life on the theatrical stage, but lived on a different stage before the church's altar. She no longer walked the streets of Hollywood, as she now resided at the Regina Laudis abbey in rural Connecticut. Hart, at the age of 74, wrote her memoir titled *The Ear of the Heart*, a memoir written fifty years after she surrendered sequined gowns for a nun's habit. In that memoir she answered the question everyone has been asking: surrendering wealth for poverty, forsaking pleasure for celibacy, leaving the limelight for candlelight. Her answer was as simple as it was profound, "If you heard what I hear, you would come too."

Mandatum

Today is Maundy Thursday and the end of Lent that began on Ash Wednesday forty days ago. These forty days were intended to be a time of self-reflection and spiritual renewal as one prepares himself or herself for Good Friday and Easter Sunday. In the early church, on Ash Wednesday, if you recall from my sermon on that day, those Christians who committed grave faults were forced to wear sackcloth and be sprinkled with ashes. They were turned out of the Christian community the same as when Adam and Eve were turned out of the Garden of Eden for their transgressions. During those forty days they were to reflect and do penance. On Maundy Thursday, today, the day on which we celebrate the Lord's Supper, they are allowed once again back into the Christian community, reconciled with the Lord and with their brothers and sisters in Christ.

For those penitents who were readmitted to the church they followed the liturgy of Exmologesis. *Exmologesis* in the Greek means "confession." Exmologesis was the penitential rite of public confession that was practiced in the early church.

During this rite those who came before the congregation could not stand, but had to kneel in humility and penance. Men were required to cut their hair and shave their beards in token of sorrow. Females were to appear with their hair disheveled and wearing a veil as an expression of their sorrow. There was no expression of joy or pleasure during this liturgy, but instead there were only tears and other expressions of grief.

With the closing of the Exmologesis liturgy, the church was once again a single body of believers. The church was once again an expression of a single unity, the Body of Christ, which is the theological message of the Lord's Supper.

On Maundy Thursday it is important to revisit Paul's message to the Corinthians, for his message is one of reconciliation. Paul's message is that the church must be a single coherent unity that is representative of being the Body of Christ.

In the Corinthian church there was apostasy, which is a renunciation of one's religious beliefs. There was debauchery, which is living a life of extreme indulgence in sensual behavior. But in this section of Paul's letter that we read as our epistle reading this morning, Paul is concerned that there are factions within the congregation. Those factions are distorting the unity of the church as well as violating the meaning of the Lord's Supper.

In the first-century church the Lord's Supper was the central act of worship, which actually incorporated a full meal. The service would begin with the blessing, breaking, and then the distribution of the bread. This would be followed by a meal. At the conclusion of the meal there would be the blessing and distribution of the wine. This was a common feast that was to be shared equally by all.

But, for the Corinthian church that was no longer the case. Those who arrived early began to eat and get drunk before those who had to travel further arrived. Also, those who arrived early and those who had more money would eat too much, leaving little or no food for those who traveled further and for those who were poor. Paul wrote that the meal that was supposed to be, in the Greek, *kurakon diepnon*, or a common meal, had become *idiom diepnon*, or a series of private meals. In the Greek *diepnon* means "banquet."

In the Corinthian church the Lord's Supper was no longer a sign of unity, but a sign of disunity. In the Corinthian church the Lord's Supper was no longer a service of harmony, but had become a service of disharmony. In the Corinthian church the Lord's Supper was no longer a liturgical practice of equality, but became an overt practice of inequality. It was a service that was no longer inclusive.

As could be well understood, Paul could not tolerate this nor could Paul allow it to continue. Addressing this issue in his letter, Paul once again instructed the church in Corinth of the proper liturgical practice of administering the Lord's Supper. It was a lesson that would be good for us to be reintroduced to again today.

It may surprise you to know that in all the letters that Paul wrote he made only two references to the public ministry of Jesus — those being, during Holy Week, Jesus' institution of the Lord's Supper in the Upper Room on Thursday and his crucifixion on Friday. All of the other references that Paul makes to Jesus in his letters are regarding the theological implications of his birth, death, and resurrection.

In our epistle reading this morning, from 1 Corinthians 11:23-26, we have the earliest recorded liturgy of the Lord's Supper as practiced by the first-century church. We also have the earliest spoken words by Jesus as recorded in our Bible.

We must keep in mind that Paul wrote about twenty years before the first gospel writer, so Paul does have the earliest historical account of the Lord's Supper. The gospel writers recount the meal that Jesus had with his disciples; whereas Paul recounts the Lord's Supper as it was practiced in the first century church. Paul, writing about 25 years after the resurrection, was a celebrant in this liturgy of the first-century church. Thus, his account of the liturgy is accurate and true to form. The liturgy that Paul transcribed in his letter was to show the meaning of the Lord's Supper as a common meal that was shared within the worshiping congregation.

The Lord's Supper is also known as Holy Communion, or a fellowship meal, once again signifying the sense of unity. The Lord's Supper is often referred to in the Greek as a Eucharist meal. Eucharist means "thanksgiving." It is a thanksgiving that remembers, confesses, and proclaims what Jesus has done.

Paul recorded the liturgical words "as often," or some translations say "whenever," which means the church frequently held the service of the Lord's Supper, we just do not know how frequent that was, be it daily or weekly.

In the liturgy Paul wrote that we are called to remember. The important word here is remember. We are to remember the death and resurrection of Jesus. In the Greek the word used for remembering is *anamnesis*. Remembering here is not individualistic, such as a person remembering their high school graduation. But remembering, as Paul uses it, is a corporate act experienced by everyone. Remembering would mean attending your class reunion, which is a corporate experience shared with other graduates.

Through corporate ritual performed in a worship service, the Lord's Super allows us to remember the passion of our Lord as a Christian community. Every time the church, together, as one body in unity, practices the Lord's Supper, we are remembering together the life, death, and resurrection of Jesus. This is why the Christians in Corinth are violating the meaning of the Lord's Supper, for it has become for them a private rather than a corporate meal.

And what is it that we remember and proclaim? It is the bread, the Body of Christ broken for us, and the cup, the blood of Christ shed for us. We are to remember and proclaim the death and resurrection of Jesus.

I guess the question for us now is this — is their unity in our congregation? Those who have been sent out with sackcloth and ashes have now returned. They have knelt before us in sorrow, but have we truly forgiven and accepted them? We must ask — does grace and forgiveness abound in our congregation or judgment and ridicule? Are we willing to accept people with different ideas and opinions? Are we willing to be tolerant and accepting?

In a short time we will be coming to the altar to receive the Lord's Supper. We are instructed in Matthew's gospel with these words, "Therefore, if you are offering your gift at the altar and there remember that your brother or sister has something against you, leave your gift there in front of the altar. First go and be reconciled to them; then come and offer your gift."

Look around the congregation. Is there someone you have offended that you need to apologize to? Is there someone whom you have viciously gossiped about? Is there someone who you have been openly harsh to? Is there someone who you still hold a grudge against? Has anyone done anything really that bad as to cause you to be unremorsefully vindictive? Was the individual really that offensive or are you just being spiteful? Does your sense of revenge trump any noble disposition? Is the real reason that you just don't like that person? Is there any place in the church for this kind of venomous attitude and behavior? Can you come to the altar without first seeking reconciliation with that individual?

Remember, Paul was directing his letter to the Christians within the Corinthian congregation and not to those outside the church. Look to the individuals in the pews that surround you, not to anyone beyond the walls of this sanctuary. Who in this sanctuary must you make amends to? And if you answer no one, then beware of the awful ugly sin of self-righteousness. If you say no one, then perhaps you need to once again put on sackcloth and cover yourself in ashes and return again in another forty days.

This day we are celebrating Maundy Thursday. It is the first and oldest service for the public reconciliation of penitents back into the fellowship of the church. This also may come as a surprise, but it is also the oldest service associated with Holy Week. This service, perhaps more than any other, is a service of forgiveness and acceptance. It is the service where you and I, sinners, are forgiven and accepted back into the church. It is the service where you and I, who have experienced grace, accept sinners back into the fellowship of the church.

Maundy Thursday comes from the Latin word *mandatum*, meaning mandate. The mandatum, that we are observing today was given to us by Jesus in the Upper Room as he shared the first meal that became known as the Lord's Supper. The mandate, the commandment, is well known to us when Jesus said at the conclusion of the meal, "I give you a new commandment: love one another. As I have loved you, so you also should love one another." To love one another is truly the hallmark of the church.

Life is difficult and people come to church to find an oasis in the desert of life. Will they find that the well is dry because those who have arrived early have consumed all the water until they are drunk? Or, will those who arrive late from the desert of life, arriving tired and exhausted, hot and sweaty, from the burdens and anxieties and woes of life and find a well that is full of clean and fresh water. Will they find that you are there to dip a cup for them.

Are we a congregation of private meals or a congregation of what the church is best known for the covered dish dinner?

Maundy Thursday is also known as Shere Thursday. Shere, spelled s-h-e-r-e, in Old English means to make "bright." It means on Maundy Thursday the dark vestments of Lent will soon be replaced by the bright vestments of Easter. On this day we prepare ourselves for a new beginning.

Shere also means to "clean" or to "wash." It comes from the act of Jesus washing the disciples' feet before the meal on this day. Because Shere Thursday is always in the Spring, the tradition of spring cleaning comes from this. If I may be sexist for a moment — housewives did you know that when you vacuumed today you were performing a liturgical act? But on this day of reconciliation, we are to clean ourselves of all sin and be brightened by the coming thought of Easter.

Foot washing is an important observance on Maundy Thursday. Jesus washed the feet of the twelve disciples as a sign of humility and service. The significance of this ritual is far reaching as it is considered by the early church as the act that instituted the priesthood of his disciples. With this act of humility the disciples were consecrated as priests to continue the ministry of Jesus after his death. This act went beyond the giving of the keys of the kingdom to Peter, for all the disciples were to be priests, and this is the forebear of ordination as we know it today.

Though you may not be ordained, you are a priest, and on this day of reconciliation you, in all humility, are to wash the feet of one another. It is a sign of forgiveness and acceptance. It is a communal act of unity.

With this service on Maundy Thursday we begin the Easter Triduum, the three holiest days of the church. It begins at sundown on Maundy Thursday, includes Good Friday, and concludes with vespers on Easter Sunday. After this service the altar will be stripped bare in mourning and will not be covered again until Easter. We begin a time of darkness that will soon be bright.

We remember this experience together, corporately, as the Body of Christ, the church.

Pontifex

Jesse Owens panicked. How could he owe $114,000 in back taxes? Soon there would be a court trial sentencing him to a long prison term. This was an issue Owens realized he had to accept, failing to personally oversee his business ventures; but instead, allowing other individuals to do it for him. He had not scrutinized the character of the men who represented him, wrongly trusting his business partners to file his personal income tax returns.

Ashamed, afraid, and anxious, Owens grabbed his jacket and rushed into the kitchen to kiss Ruth, his wife, good-bye. Not even pausing to explain where he was going, and in a rush that can only be caused by panic, he took the stairs out of the house three and four at a time, as he yelled over his shoulder that he would be back tomorrow. Half an hour later he was at Chicago's O'Hare Airport with a round-trip ticket to his boyhood home in Alabama.

Oakville was no longer a community of fields maintained by share croppers. Over the years Oakville had developed into a town. Buildings now stood in place of pastures. Despondent by the lack of familiar landmarks, Owens worried that he would never be able to find that plot of earth where his family's shack once stood. Frantically, he ran about the town, darting here, dashing there, zigzagging his way across town, desperate to find that place he once called home. Then somehow he just knew... he just knew... he was standing on the spot where he once lived. The 53-year-old man, an Olympic track and gold medal athlete, fell to his knees. He dug his hands into the dirt that he and his family once farmed, and he started to pray. He prayed in such agony that he sensed only one last drop of blood was left in his spirit. Then he realized, "True prayer means nothing else but giving the final drop of your soul's blood to reach God."

At some point all of us are going to find ourselves in a seemingly hopeless and helpless situation. The problem, we believe, exceeds our emotional and physical resources. Other times we will be consumed by the guilt of our sin and the mismanagement of our lives, thinking there can be no redemption for our wayward soul. The situation confronting us seemingly defies a solution. Apprehensive, we await our doom.

Condemnation would be our precarious lot except we have a high priest who has taken upon himself our sin, our guilt, our remorse, the problems of our own making. When we confront these problems that defy description and are overwhelmed by a transgression that leaves us numb, there is a sense of security and well-being in knowing that Jesus is our high priest who guides and forgives us. The trials and tribulations of life will not subdue us, for we have Jesus as our pastor.

It is only in the book of Hebrews that the christological title of high priest is applied to Jesus, which is reflected in our lectionary reading for this morning. Our lesson says we have a "great priest over the house of God." Earlier in Hebrews the author writes, "Therefore, since we have a great high priest who has ascended into heaven, Jesus the Son of God, let us hold firmly to the faith we profess. For we do not have a high priest who is unable to empathize with our weaknesses, but we have one who has been tempted in every way, just as we are — yet he did not sin. Let us then approach God's throne of grace with confidence, so that we may receive mercy and find grace to help us in our time of need." Jesus, our great high priest, can emphasize with the trials and tribulations that confront us.

Jesus, that great high priest, was alongside Jesse Owens digging his fingers into the farmland of Oakville, Alabama.

The author of Hebrews remains unknown and who wrote the book has been strongly debated through the centuries. There is very strong evidence that Hebrews was written by a woman, perhaps Priscilla. This would make Hebrews the only book in the Bible penned by a female. I like the idea that a woman wrote at least one book of the Bible, so until it can be proven otherwise I accept Priscilla as the author.

In Hebrews we learn that on the cross this Good Friday Jesus became the great high priest over the house of God. This declaration makes the priestly ministry of God available to everyone, as it is no longer confined to the legalism of Judaism.

In the Jewish temple in Jerusalem, in the inner sanctum was the Holy of Holies. The Holy of Holies was twenty cubits long, twenty cubits wide, and forty cubits high. The floor, walls, and ceiling were all plated with gold. The entrance was covered with a veil, which was overlaid with gold and had sockets of silver. The curtain itself was woven into four colors: white, blue, scarlet, and purple. Inside the Holy of Holies rested the ark of the covenant that housed the tablets of the Ten Commandments.

On the Day of Atonement, which occurred only once a year, only the high priest would be permitted to enter the Holy of Holies. As no one else was ever allowed to enter this sanctuary, a rope was tied around the high priest for if he would become ill or die he could be pulled out.

The atonement ritual began centuries earlier with Aaron, and was ritualistic followed by the subsequent high priests of Israel. The solemnity of the day was underscored by God telling Moses to warn Aaron not to come into the most holy place whenever he felt like it, lest he die. It was only on the Day of Atonement, this special observance recognized only once a year, that the high priest could enter the most holy place. Before entering the tabernacle, the high priest would bathe and put on special garments. He would then sacrifice a bull as a sin offering for himself and his family. The blood of the bull was sprinkled on the ark. Then the high priest would bring forth two goats. The first goat would be sacrificed because of the uncleanness and rebellion of the Israelites, with its blood sprinkled on the ark. The second goat was used as a scapegoat. The high priest placed his hands on its head, confessed over it the disobedience and wickedness of the Israelites. Then the scapegoat would be led away into the wilderness and put to death by being thrown down a rocky precipice. The scapegoat carried on itself all the sins of the people, which were forgiven for another year.

And it is from this religious act we get our term today that when we wrongly blame someone for causing our faults, the individual becomes for us a scapegoat.

Priscilla, in our lesson this morning, declared that Jesus was the embodiment of the new high priest whose act of atonement was both final and complete.

The early church realized that upon the cross Jesus became the high priest and the temple ritual was no longer valid. It is written by the gospel writers, "And when Jesus had cried out again in a loud voice, he gave up his spirit. At that moment the curtain of the temple was torn in two from top to bottom." The temple curtain was now torn top to bottom symbolizing that any person, not just the high priest, but any individual, could freely and voluntarily approach the altar of forgiveness.

The Latin word for "priest" is *pontifex*, which means "bridge-builder." Jesus is now the bridge-builder. Jesus himself is the bridge between man and God. He is the high priest who intercedes on our behalf.

Martin Luther, the father of the Protestant Reformation of the sixteenth century, was always fearful of the state of his soul, fearing it to be condemned to hell for his lack of obedience to the rituals of the Roman Catholic church. No matter how dedicated he was to the required offices of being both a priest and a monk, he feared that salvation had always escaped him, and at best he would be assigned to purgatory upon his death.

To amend his sins he made a pilgrimage to Rome. In the holy city he embarked upon every ritual of redemption sanctioned by the Vatican. One such appointment was climbing Pilate's stairs, 28 marble steps, on hand and knees, kissing each one while reciting the *Pater Noster*, which is Latin name for our Lord's Prayer. Each one of the 28 marble steps acted as an indulgence that would lessen one's time in purgatory.

Luther elected not to engage in this exercise for himself, but for another. Luther directed that his indulgences be for Grandpa Heine, that his time spent in purgatory would be lessened.

Having completed the legalistic ritual, at the top of the steps Luther raised himself to his feet and in disillusionment of what he had just done and exclaimed, "Who knows whether it is so?"

It is a question of who could possibly know if this made any difference in releasing a soul from purgatory. Luther further doubted that kneeling on 29 marble steps could be an effective method for personal forgiveness. One may have a feeling of self-righteousness for completing such a grueling task, but did it really refresh the soul Luther questioned? For we know that forgiveness comes only through confession. This is why climbing Pilate's stairs was one of Luther's final acts before declaring the Protestant theological doctrine of justification by grace alone, coupled with the denouncement of the Roman Catholic view of works-righteousness.

Jesus became the high priest on the cross on Good Friday. We know that Jesus was sinless, but on the cross he experienced sin. On that cross he experienced the feeling of sin and the pain of estrangement from God. When Jesus on the cross uttered the words, "My God, my God, why hast thou forsaken me?" he experienced the same pain and forsakenness of being separated from God as you and I do when we feel separated from our creator due to our sin, disobedience, and doubts. Though Jesus was still without sin, he experienced the agony you and I endure each moment we separate ourselves from God because of our sin. At this moment Jesus became our high priest.

Jesus, as the high priest, now experienced the agony of digging one's fingers into the soil of Oakville, Alabama. Jesus, as the high priest, knew that crawling up 28 marble steps did not offer one's soul the cleansing that only confession can. On the cross Jesus became our high priest who understands and shares in our sufferings.

Jesus became our "priest," our *pontifex*, our bridge-builder between us and God. The temple curtain has been torn asunder and now Jesus our high priest personally brings us before the altar of God. The blood of a bull is no longer needed. A scapegoat no longer needs to be driven off the side of a cliff. For now we can enter the golden room absent of any rope tied about our waist.

This is the message of Good Friday. Good Friday does have the message of salvation embedded in it, but the message of the cross goes so far beyond that. The message of Good Friday is the one who could say "My God, my God, why hast thou forsaken me?" knows our sorrows and shame. Jesus understanding and being able to relate to our transgressions, he becomes the new high priest of comfort and redemption. As Jesus looks down upon us from that cross bar we know he will minister unto us. And as we look up at the cross, and in the Roman Catholic tradition we see Jesus still nailed to that cross bar, we know we are to go forth and be a priest unto others.

Mary Edwards Walker is the only woman to be awarded the Medal of Honor. She was fortunate to have parents who encouraged her independence, free thinking, and the importance of receiving an education. Because of her parents support and her own tenacity she graduated in 1855 with a medical degree from Syracuse Medical College in New York. She was the only woman in her graduating class.

When the Civil War began she volunteered as a doctor and was present at the First Battle of Bull Run. But as prejudice prevailed in the military, Walker was forbidden to be a physician, she could only fulfill the duties of a nurse. As the war progressed, and as she was present at more battles, she was finally made the first female physician in the Army, assigned to the 52nd Ohio Infantry in the Army of the Cumberland. Walker put no limits on herself for providing medical care. She tended to the wounded in the hospitals, she would administer aid on the field of battle, and she would even cross over Confederate lines in order to treat a wounded soldier.

On April 10, 1864, just after she assisted a Confederate doctor with an amputation, she was arrested. She was sent to the Castle Thunder prison camp in Richmond, Virginia. On August 12 she was released from prison as a part of a prisoner exchange for a Confederate surgeon from Tennessee that the Union had captured.

After the war Walker continued to practice medicine, but because female doctors were not trusted she had difficulty getting patients. She was also very involved in the abolitionist, feminist, and prohibition movements.

On the recommendation of General William Tecumseh and General George Henry Thomas, Mary Edwards Walker was awarded the Medal of Honor. She received the award for her willingness to treat soldiers on the field of battle, but even more so for the courage of crossing enemy lines to administer medical care.

We learn this day — this Good Friday — the message of the cross is that we are all to be a high priest, we are all bridge-builders, we are the *pontifex* that will make any sacrifice to promote the well-being of another individual.

The Sawdust Trail

Presbyterian minister Reverend Benjamin Weir, in his book *Hostage Bound, Hostage Free*, reveals what it was like to be held hostage. He was captured on the streets of Beirut by a group of Shiite Muslim extremists, in May, 1984. Weir was imprisoned for sixteen months. During those torturous months he was often chained and held in solitary confinement. Weir's devout faith and trust in God sustained him during those perilous times.

One routine in particular sustained Weir's reliance on Jesus. Weir realized that if he dared to stand on the toilet, always in fear of being caught, he could look out the window. Doing so, he could see beyond the Bekaa Valley to the Lebanon Mountains. The snow covered mountains and rays of early morning sunlight strengthened his faith. Weir confessed, "That sight, and the memory of it throughout the day, spoke to me of the grandeur of the Creator and his good intensions for the world and its people. This gave me hope and a sense of harmony."

Many things in life hold us hostage, whether it is an addiction to drugs, alcohol, tobacco, money, sex, television, workaholic or a hobby out-of-control. In our daily living we feel ourselves in bondage to pain, health problems, grief, difficult decisions, unruly neighbors, inconsiderate coworkers, and an uncompromising boss. For all these problems and others, each robbing life of its joy and satisfaction, we call upon the name of Jesus for help.

This is why our lectionary Easter lesson for this morning is so very important. Paul wrote, "So if you have been raised with Christ, seek the things that are above, where Christ is, seated at the right hand of God. Set your minds on things that are above, not on things that are on earth."

It would be wrong to say just looking to things above, just looking to Christ above, and your problems will be solved. This would be wrong for it would deny the real problems we suffer in life. It would be wrong for it would trivialize any hardship that we are enduring. It would be wrong for it would imply that just believing in Jesus will make every disparity in life evaporate. And we know that will not happen.

No matter how many times Benjamin Weir stood on that toilet seat looking out the window, he was still in prison. He had no idea of a release date, or even if there would be one. But yet, it was looking beyond the Bekaa Valley to the Lebanon Mountains that sustained him, it gave him hope, it gave him the energy, it gave him a reason to get up in the morning.

What Paul is saying to us is that once we have died with Christ and then have been risen with Christ, our hope is found in heavenly places. We are to live in this earthly world realizing that it is fraught with problems; yet, if by faith we can keep our focus on the resurrected Lord we can endure.

J. Philip Wogaman was the professor of Christian ethics at Wesley Theological Seminary in Washington DC. He later became the senior pastor of Foundry United Methodist Church in Washington DC. Wogaman's name may be more familiar with you as the Clinton's and the Bush's often worshiped at Foundry when he was the pastor.

When Dr. Wogaman taught ethics at Wesley he would begin the first class of each new semester by asking the same question: "What is the central theme of the Bible?" And each semester he got his traditional expected answers, with salvation and love always ranking the highest. Dr. Wogaman would then startle the class when he informed the students that the central theme of the Bible is hope.

In the Bible every story of obedience, every story of faith, is a story of hope. It is the belief that somehow, however unseemingly, God will prevail. And on this Easter Sunday, we know that the ultimate testimony to hope is the resurrection. The resurrection gives us the hope that God is ultimately in control and will prevail, if not now then at the end times. It is for this reason Paul tells us that we can look to the things that are above and not be held captive to earthly problems and desires.

One of the most important Bible verses we have for Easter Sunday is recorded in the gospel of John when Jesus said, "I am the resurrection and the life. Those who believe in me, even though they die, will live, and everyone who lives and believes in me will never die." Believe in the power of Jesus. Jesus can and will change your life for the better. With Jesus life will become a more enriching and rewarding experience. In the name of Jesus you can surmount the problems of daily living.

This is one of the "I am" sayings of Jesus. There are 54 "I am" sayings in the fourth gospel. In John's gospel when Jesus uses "I am" in an absolute sense, he is identifying himself with God. In the Greek the word *eimi* is translated as "I am." *Eimi* means "to be" or "to exist eternally" or "to have timeless being." Thus, the "I am" saying declares the eternal nature of Jesus and his oneness with God.

Jesus declaration, "I am the resurrection and the life," is spoken only once in the New Testament. It is a part of the story of when Jesus learned that his good friend Lazarus, who was the brother of Mary and Martha, had died. Jesus, on the road, two miles from the city of Bethany, encountered the sisters and learned of the sad news. Further, he was chastised for not being present to heal the one they so dearly loved. Approaching the tomb, Jesus was so overcome with grief the scriptures reported, "Jesus began to weep." Jesus then called forth Lazarus from the tomb.

Jesus is recorded in the fourth gospel as saying: "I am the light of the world." "I am the good shepherd." "I am the way, the truth, and the life." "I am the door." "I am the true vine." "I am the resurrection and the life." These "I am" sayings may best tell us who Jesus is on this Easter day and what Paul means for us to "set your minds on things that are above."

On September 17, 1942 Colonel Leslie R. Groves was selected to oversee the Manhattan Project. The purpose of this project was to develop the world's first atomic bomb. Even though the assignment came with a promotion to brigadier general, Groves was disappointed with the appointment. Yearning for overseas duty, he was disgruntled by the prospect of filling a trivial administrative position in Washington DC. Besides, the project held little promise for success. Groves, utterly frustrated, realized: an inadequate supply of uranium had been mined; scientists were still uncertain about the chemical properties of plutonium; production equipment had yet to be designed; acquisitions for plant sites were in abeyance; and the entire nuclear process was only a theory. Perturbed, Groves judged, "The whole endeavor was founded on possibilities rather than probabilities." But it was in the midst of those possibilities that the A-bomb was created.

Frequently it is "possibilities" and not "probabilities" that propel us forward toward our goal. We are sustained by the belief that it can be done. And is not the meaning of possibilities almost synonymous with the word hope. And is not the message of the Resurrection that if we live by faith we live by possibilities.

I am cautious not to confuse possibilities with the prosperity gospel for the possibilities that we seek do not have any kind of material reward attached to them. The prosperity gospel encourages people to look for things on earth, and Paul is very clear our focus must be heavenly.

Paul goes on in Colossians to list those earthly things that we must surrender. Paul wrote: "Put to death, therefore, whatever belongs to your earthly nature: sexual immorality, impurity, lust, evil desires and greed, which is idolatry. But now you must also rid yourselves of all such things as these: anger, rage, malice, slander, and filthy language from your lips. Do not lie to each other."

We could discuss each item on Paul's list, but there is really no need to. We are all very well aware of how these vices can destroy lives and relationships. We are probably aware of their destructive nature because each of us has found ourselves dwelling between the quotation marks on his list of a sinful life.

As sinners, we need to be sure that we are only renters and have not taken up permanent residence on that list. But before we can leave our rented apartment where we sin and hope no on one sees we need to hear a strong uncompromising evangelical message on sin and judgment.

Billy Sunday was a professional baseball player from 1883 to 1891 for teams in Chicago, Pittsburgh and Philadelphia. He was converted through the street preaching of Harry Monroe of the Pacific Garden Mission in Chicago. He left a $5,000 a year salary as a baseball player for a $75 yearly salary as a YMCA evangelist. He was an evangelist from 1893 to 1935. Sunday is known for his theatrical preaching that was filled with baseball imagery. He would wind up like a pitcher and slam a fist into his other hand as he threw a "fastball at the devil." To demonstrate a sinner coming home for salvation he would slide headfirst on the floor, groping with his hand for home plate. Going forward and clasping Billy's hand at the end of the service was known as "hitting the sawdust trail," as most tabernacle floors were covered with sawdust. It is estimated that several hundred-thousand people walked "the sawdust trail."

His sermons, as with so many other evangelists of his day, focused on the degenerate state of men and women. In his sermon, "The Devil's Boomerangs," Sunday opened with this oration: "You can always get the truth out of the Bible. You can always find truth elsewhere, but never from so clear a source. Nothing was ever printed more true than 'Whatsoever a man soweth, that shall he reap.' God will not coerce and attempt to force any man to be a Christian. When he dies, however, he will be judged for his sins. He must face the day of judgment. Do as you please — lie, steal, booze, fight, prostitute. God won't stop you. Do as you please until the undertaker comes and puts you in a coffin and then the Lord will have his say. Lives of pleasure shall have an end, the wicked shall not live half their days."

With these words Sunday began a litany against every carnal sin known to humanity. We need to take seriously Billy Sunday's condemnation of sin and perhaps be a bit more receptive to his descriptive language of judgment if we are to surrender our earthly ways of living.

Paul, being an established theologian, also informs us in Colossians what it means to set our minds on those things which are above. Paul lists these as: "clothe yourselves with compassion, kindness, humility, gentleness and patience. Bear with each other and forgive one another... And over all these virtues put on love, which binds them all together in perfect unity."

The theological bases of our lectionary lesson this morning is that we have died with Christ, and now we have risen with Christ. It would be very appropriate to quote Paul from Galatians when he writes, "I have been crucified with Christ and I no longer live, but Christ lives in me. The life I now live in the body, I live by faith in the Son of God, who loved me and gave himself for me."

To live with Christ within is to clothe one's self with compassion, kindness, humility, gentleness, patience, and love. I wonder if any us can comprehend what life would be like if our homes, our church, our workplace, our hobby center were all clothed with compassion, kindness, humility, gentleness, patience, and love.

Up to the 1960s Easter Sunday was the day everyone wore a new outfit. And I think it was less out of vanity and more out of celebration. It was recognition of just how special Easter is to the Christian community and to worshiping congregation.

Perhaps now it is time for us to wear our Easter outfits everywhere we go, even mowing the grass. Perhaps it is time for us to wear kindness even when we are most irritated — to wear patience when we know we could make this all go faster. Perhaps it is time for us to wear gentleness when confronted with someone who is disagreeable. The situations in which we should clothe ourselves with compassion, kindness, humility, gentleness, patience, and love are endless. And we know it. We just have to do it.

Thomas Alva Edison was never defeated by failure. After 50,000 unsuccessful attempts at developing the nickel-iron-alkaline battery, a friend asked the esteemed inventor if he were disillusioned. "Not at all," Edison encouragingly replied, "for I have learned 50,000 ways it cannot be done and therefore I am fifty thousand times nearer the final successful experiment." Eventually the battery was developed. Edison was a genius, and a large part of his genius was knowing that he would never yield to disappointment.

Let us take up the challenge of 50,000 attempts to clothe ourselves with compassion, kindness, humility, gentleness, patience, and love.

Sola Fide

Peter was so excited about his new life in Christ that he opened this section of his letter with a doxology. He began this section of his letter with this verse from a doxology, "Blessed be the God and Father of our Lord Jesus Christ!"

Doxologies have always been a part of worship, with the earliest form dating back to Solomon. But the doxologies used in Jewish worship were given a new meaning in Christian worship. In Judaism the doxology was sung to a God who is distant and remote. The Jews would sing these words in their Jewish doxology, "Blessed art thou, O God." The Christians, realizing the Messiah had come, sang a doxology to a God who was intimate and personal because God had been made known to them by Jesus. Peter related the Christian doxology to a very personal God as we hear these words, "Blessed be the God and Father of our Lord Jesus Christ!" Notice the difference. In Judaism the doxology blesses God. In Christian worship the doxology blesses a very personal God, as they sing to God who is the Father of Jesus.

A doxology may be found in almost every book in the New Testament. They were used because they were easily recognized by the readers of the book and the message of the doxology was universally understood, so no interpretation was needed on the part of the author. Since the message of the doxology was so well understood in the Christian community, the author by just quoting a verse from a doxology would help bring clarity to the message he wanted to convey in the rest of his epistle.

The word doxology comes from two Greek words, *doxa* and *logos*, which means "words of praise." A doxology contains words of praise sung to God. When we sing a doxology in worship it is a very sacred moment.

Doxologies were composed to express a theological doctrine of the church. The doxology we sing today has not changed since the fourth century. The early church had many heretical groups that distorted established orthodox theology. A very prominent heresy in the fourth century was Arianism. Arianism would not acknowledge the full divinity of Christ nor would it acknowledge the full divinity of the Holy Spirit. Basically, Arianism refused to believe that Jesus and the Holy Spirit were equal expressions of God.

The doxology we sing in worship today, the Gloria Patri, was made the official statement of orthodox theology for the church at the Edict of Thessalonica of 380. It was composed specifically to disavow the beliefs promoted by the Armenians. The words of the Gloria Patri should be familiar to us:

Glory be to the Father, and to the Son: and to the Holy Ghost;
As it was in the beginning, is now, and ever shall be: world without end. Amen.

The Gloria Patri affirms the Trinity that God and Jesus and the Holy Spirit were together at the beginning of creation and are equal representatives of God.

I hope that when we come to worship this first Sunday after our great Easter celebration, and for every Sunday in the months to follow, that we have the same excitement for our faith as Peter expressed in choosing to begin this section of his letter with a verse from a doxology. It is a verse that tells us that our God is both majestic and intimate.

Peter had a good reason to be excited because he knew Jesus personally. That is why he wanted everyone to sing a doxology of praise to a majestic and intimate God that he knew personally. This was a personal relationship because Peter walked with Jesus and ate meals with Jesus.

Peter, before Jesus changed his name, was known as Simon. Simon was an ordinary fisherman in Galilee. Simon was married and the foundation of his home can still be seen in Israel today. When Simon and his brother Andrew were summoned by Jesus to be two of his twelve disciples they immediately left their fishing boats to become a part of Jesus ministry. Simon soon became the leader of the twelve and for this reason Jesus changed his name to Peter, which in the Greek is *petra* or rock.

Even though Peter was the rock of the group, the rock had a fault line in it. This is best recalled when we remember that Peter denied knowing Jesus three times in the garden during Jesus' trial. When Peter realized what he had done he was deeply shamed, and wept bitterly. But it was Peter who was the first disciple that Jesus appeared to after his resurrection. And on that seashore next to the morning breakfast being roasted on an open fire, Peter was asked by Jesus three times to reaffirm his faith, which Peter readily did. Peter was the first to preach on the Day of Pentecost, and from that experience Peter embarked on missionary journeys.

This was the Peter who was so excited about Jesus that he wanted the world to know Jesus. This was the Peter who wanted us to sing a doxology of praise to Jesus.

Peter's love and dedication to Jesus may best be understood by how he died. Peter was in Rome when Emperor Nero began persecuting the church in the year 64. Peter was arrested, imprisoned, and sentenced to death by crucifixion. Peter demanded that he be crucified upside down for he did not feel worthy to be crucified right side up as his Lord was.

The importance of singing the doxology and the significance of reviewing Peter's life comes with this line that Peter wrote in his letter, "Although you have not seen him, you love him; and even though you do not see him now, you believe in him and rejoice with an incredible and glorious joy."

Peter wrote of his excitement of having personally known Jesus. Peter was able to walk the dusty roads with

Jesus. Peter was present when Jesus taught and healed. Peter had the privilege of knowing those things that are not recorded in the scriptures; such as those conversations around the campfire at night. Peter suffered through observing the crucifixion, but Peter was also part of the glorious witness to the resurrection.

Peter was saying in his letter how wonderful it was that those who never knew Jesus personally could still believe in Jesus and sing a doxology of praise. You and I, sitting in this sanctuary, are those Christians who have not seen Jesus in the flesh, but still believe and rejoice.

When Jesus spoke to Doubting Thomas, Jesus was speaking directly to us in this sanctuary this day. Jesus said to Thomas, "Because you have seen me, you have believed; blessed are those who have not seen and yet have believed."

Thomas was called Doubting Thomas because when he learned that Jesus was resurrected he questioned how true the story was. Thomas wanted proof. Instead of calling Thomas the doubter, perhaps he should be known as the questioner. Thomas did not doubt the integrity of those who saw the resurrected Jesus, but let's be honest, the story was so preposterous that it would cause someone to ask questions. Thomas wanted to authenticate the story for himself and not just take someone else's word for it. The proof for Thomas was that Thomas wanted to touch the nail wounds. Jesus then did appear to Thomas in the Upper Room. We know that Jesus showed Thomas his nail wounds, but we do not know if Thomas actually touched the wounds. The question is: Was just seeing Jesus enough for Thomas to believe?

Thomas was among the few like those in the Upper Room, in the garden, on the road to Emmaus, by the seashore, who actually physically saw the resurrected Jesus. For those who followed in the days, weeks, months, years, and even centuries after these encounters with the risen Lord, as Jesus said to Thomas he says to us this morning, "blessed are those who have not seen and yet have believed."

There will never be any physical proof that Jesus walked the earth because those who come to believe this day do so only by faith. Once we have physical proof of Jesus then Christianity is no longer a religion whose only base for authenticity is faith.

We believe in the witness of Peter. We believe in the testimony of the New Testament. We believe in the writings of the early church fathers. We believe in what our family and friends have told us. But ultimately we believe because within us we had this mysterious spiritual conviction that Jesus did die for our sins, was resurrected, and ascended to heaven.

Martin Luther, the founder of Protestantism in the sixteenth century, established perhaps the Protestants' primary theological doctrine — *sola fide,* which in Latin means "by faith alone." Luther considered the Bible as our ultimate authority whose message declares that we can now live by the promise of "by faith alone." We are saved by faith alone and not by good works. We need to do good works, but these good actions are only an expression of our faith and fellowship with Jesus.

The doctrine set forth by Luther has continually been confirmed by the church. The Genevan Confession was written by the reformer John Calvin in 1536 likewise pointed out the necessity of those justified live by faith. It reads, "We confess that the entrance which we have to the great treasures and riches of the goodness of God that *vouchsafed* us is by faith; inasmuch as, in certain confidence and assurance of heart, we believe in the promises of the gospel." The Geneva Confession says we enter into a relationship with Jesus by faith. We have confidence in our relationship with Jesus because of the assurance of our heart and because we believe in the promises of the Bible.

The Westminster Confession of Faith is a Reformed confession of faith. It was adopted in 1646 at the Westminster Assembly and became the standard confession of the Church of England. Regarding *sola fide* the creed states, "Faith, thus receiving and resting on Christ and his righteousness, is the alone instrument of justification." The creed states it is by faith that we believe that Jesus died for our sins and was resurrected and ascended to heaven where he sits at the right hand of God.

It is only because we believe by faith alone that I am skeptical of any physical evidence of the existence of Jesus.

The Shroud of Turin comes most readily to mind as people trying to present physical proof that Jesus walked the roads of Israel. Many believe that it is the burial cloth of Jesus. The shroud has impressed upon it, like a photograph negative, a man. The description and positon of the man with a beard and apparent crown of thrones could lead one to believe that it is Jesus burial cloth. And many believe that this image was impressed upon the cloth when Jesus was resurrected. Many believe in the authenticity of this being the burial cloth of Jesus, even though carbon dating places the cloth between 1260 and 1390. The Roman Catholic church has neither denied nor affirmed its authenticity, but the church has designated it as an icon.*

If you have seen the movie *Risen*, Roman military tribune Clavius, a dedicated Army officer with 25 years of active service that exposed him to many battles, is ordered by Pontius Pilate to disprove the rumors that Jesus is the Jewish Messiah who had risen from the grave. In the course of the movie Clavius becomes a Christian and gives up his position in the army. But in one telling scene, Clavius in his confusion to learn the truth, is seen kneeling in the empty tomb holding the burial cloth of Jesus, which of course is an exact replica of the Shroud of Turin. So, unto an unsuspecting public, but to appease the evangelicals in the audience, Hollywood perpetuates a myth. But because we can only know the resurrected Jesus by faith, shroud of turin will never be the authentic and historical burial cloth of Jesus. Like all mysteries, science and faith are conflicted regarding its authenticity. But if the shroud is actually physical evidence of the resurrection, then Christianity would no longer be a religion based on faith alone. This is why the shroud is a hoax.

Faith and rebirth are central themes in the scriptures. It is the teaching of the need to be born again. The phrase "to be born again," which means to be saved, comes from the biblical story of Nicodemus.

You may recall the story of Nicodemus, who was a Pharisee and a member of the Sanhedrin, who comes to Jesus at night. Nicodemus came at night because of his social position in society, knowing what people would say about him if it was made public that he was taking to Jesus. Nicodemus wanted to know more about the teaching of Jesus and how one could become a follower. Jesus told Nicodemus "Truly, truly, I say to you, unless one is born again he cannot see the kingdom of God." Nicodemus took these words literally at first, inquiring, "How can a man be born when he is old? Can he enter a second time into his mother's womb and be born?" Jesus compassionately answered, "Truly, truly, I say to you, unless one is born of water and the Spirit, he cannot enter the kingdom of God." Now Nicodemus understood. To be born again is to have a spiritual rebirth. It is a spiritual rebirth where you come to accept Jesus as the Messiah by faith, and this conversation must have had an impact on Nicodemus. We are never told if Nicodemus became a Christian, but we are told that he was the only member of the Sanhedrin who defended Jesus during his trial.

It is from the story of Nicodemus that we get the Christian testimony that to be saved, to be converted, to have faith, is to be born again.

When Jimmy Carter ran for president of the United States in 1976, he would often share with the news media that he was a born again Christian. If you would watch some of the news reels from this time, anchors on major news broadcasts publically admitted they were confused by what the term "born again" meant. They did not understand that Jimmy Carter was a converted Christian who lived by faith.

Perhaps the 1976 election confusion was the fault of the church. Newscasters did not understand Jimmy Carter being born again because the church had failed in being evangelical. The church failed in being forthright on the mandate to be born again. The church failed to make every living soul know what it means to live by faith alone. And I can only ask if we are still failing in our evangelical mission this day.

I can only hope that all of us can articulate our faith with the same excitement and joy as Peter did. And though we only know Jesus spiritually, our relationship with Jesus is as real as Peter's ever was. And are we, like Peter, so dedicated to spreading the gospel message that we are willing to be crucified upside down?

If your sanctuary has a screen you may want to show a picture of the Shroud of Turin.

Surrounded by Angels

Archbishop Fulton J. Sheen was both a great scholar and a very compassionate man. Bishop Sheen taught theology and philosophy at The Catholic University of America before he was made the Bishop of Rochester in 1966,though Bishop Sheen is best known to the public for his radio and television programs. For twenty years, from 1930 to 1950, Sheen hosted the night-time radio program "The Catholic Hour." He then moved to television in 1951with the program "Life Is Worth Living." Sheen continued in television until 1968. For this work, Sheen won two Emmy awards for most outstanding television personality, and was featured on the cover of Time magazine.

Bishop Sheen often told this story on the meaning of redemption.

One evening Archbishop Sheen was dining alone in the Statler Hotel in Boston. Looking up from his meal he saw a shoeshine boy in tattered dirty rags that substituted for clothes. When the headwaiter spotted the urchin he immediately ushered the lad out of the lobby and back into the alley from whence he came. Sheen, with a sudden loss of appetite, went in search of the boy.

Finding the child, the two sat and conversed. The Archbishop learned that the boy was expelled from Catholic school for misbehavior. The boy was adamant that the verdict of the Mother Superior was final, and the school doors were permanently closed to his admittance.

The next day the Archbishop visited the Mother Superior and shared this story with her: "I know of three boys who were thrown out of religious schools: one because he was constantly drawing pictures during geography class; another because he was fond of fighting; and the third because he kept revolutionary books hidden under his mattress. No one knows the names of the valedictorians of those classes, but the first boy was Hitler, the second Mussolini, and the third Stalin. I am sure that if the superiors of those schools would have given those boys another chance, they might have turned out differently in the world. Maybe this boy will prove himself worthy if you take him back." Unable to dispute the wisdom of Fulton Sheen, the Mother Superior reinstated the boy. Upon graduation, the young man accepted a calling into the priesthood and journeyed forth as a missionary among the Eskimos.

We are all sinners desperate for a second chance. We are all sinners who desire to know the inner peace that comes with forgiveness. We are all sinners who would like to turn our lives around from drawing pictures in geography class to becoming a missionary, if not to the Eskimos at least to our own neighborhoods. This is why we confess our sins and accept Jesus as our Savior.

In Judaism the word "savior" is used in recognition of a national hero who delivered the citizens of the land from peril. In one episode of national crisis, the Hebrews were suffering unmercifully under the reign of the king of Aram. In the book of 2 Kings we read, "Therefore the LORD gave Israel a savior, so that they escaped from the hands of the Arameans..."

Rarely in Judaism is the word applied to God, but Isaiah shares with us a time of awful tribulation in Israel, and described how God became the nation's Savior. Isaiah recounts these words of the Creator, "For I am the LORD your God, the holy one of Israel, your Savior."

In the Hebrew language the root meaning for the word Savior is "helper," "preserver," or "deliverer." This message was carried into the writings of the first century Christians, who readily applied it to Jesus. In Greek, the name Jesus means "to help," "to preserve," "to save." This is why Matthew can unabashedly open his gospel confessing that God spoke to Joseph in a dream regarding his newborn with this declaration, "... and you are to name him Jesus, for he will save his people from their sins."

As recorded in Acts, the first sermon Peter preached on the Day of Pentecost he boldly declared, "Repent and be baptized, every one of you, in the name of Jesus Christ for the forgiveness of your sins. And you will receive the gift of the Holy Spirit." Peter defined the saving work of Jesus in terms of remission of sins.

As Matthew tells us, Jesus as the Savior came "to give his life as a ransom for many."

Peter in our lectionary reading for this morning continues the theological theme that we were ransomed from our sins by Jesus. Peter wrote that because of Jesus "we were ransomed from our futile ways" of living. Peter continued that we were not ransomed with perishable things like silver or gold, but, as Peter wrote we were ransomed "with the precious blood of Christ."

Jesus ransomed us from our sins because he became for us the new Paschal Lamb.

The Paschal Lamb is a symbol of sacrifice. In Judaism the killing of an unblemished lamb is embodied in all ceremonies for atonement and cleansing, as well as in most celebrations that involve a feast. The blood of the lamb is inseparable from the celebration of the Passover. Recounting the Exodus story, in order for the angel of death to pass over a Jewish home in the land of Egypt, sparing the life of the firstborn male, a lamb had to be slaughtered and the blood placed upon the seal of the door. The blood of the lamb is a symbol of deliverance.

On Friday of Holy Week Jesus was nailed to a cross atop a hill overlooking Jerusalem. At the same noon hour the priests in the temple were slitting the throat of each lamb brought to them by a pilgrim as atonement for sin. The family would then take the carcass to be cooked and eaten for the Feast. The evangelist John made it clear to all his readers that these two events happened simultaneously with this passage, "Now it was the day for the preparation of the Passover; and it was about noon. Pilate said to the Jews, 'Here is your King!'"

Why Jesus had to be crucified is often asked and debated. The discussion can now end for John provides the answer. As the priests were making sin offerings in the temple square, God was making the conclusive sin offering on the cross. As blood was shed to avenge the angel of death of the firstborn, blood was now shed for the ultimate deliverance of all God's children. Jesus was being executed at exactly the same time as the Passover lambs were being slaughtered in the temple. The priests who haughtily enforced the death of the Lamb of God recessed to the temple to commence the legalistic sacrifice of the Paschal Lambs. Beyond question, the symbolism of the two events happening simultaneously is that Jesus is God's Passover Lamb, sacrificed for the deliverance of God's people, and the legalistic temple practice has been replaced now and forever. Jesus is the culmination of the sacrificial system, never to be repeated, only to be remembered and revered. This is why Peter could confess that we were ransomed from our sins, "with the precious blood of Christ, like that of a lamb without defect or blemish."

In the liturgy of the United Methodist church participation the Lord's Supper is participating in the sacrament of reconciliation with God and one another. During the service, these stanzas can be spoken or sung by the congregation in response to the Prayer of Humble Access: "O Lamb of God, that takest away the sins of the world, have mercy upon us. O Lamb of God, that takest away the sins of the world, have mercy upon us. O Lamb of God, that takest away the sins of the world, grant us thy peace."

Peter was emphatic in wanting his readers to know how precious the ransomed blood of Christ is so we can fully understand what it means to be a Christian who can say, "O Lamb of God, that takest away the sins of the world, grant us thy peace."

Peter wrote that because we have been saved from our sins, we have experienced conversion, that is to be born again, we can now, as Peter wrote "trust in God" and have "faith and hope."

Believing in Christ grants us more than the serenity that comes with knowing our sins are forgiven and we have eternal life. It also means, as Peter tells us, we can "trust in God," and we can have a "faith and hope that are set on God."

Christianity unfortunately is not magic that once you become a believer all of your problems just disappear. Believers are still going to get ill. Believers are still going to have family problems. Believers are still going to find their work situation to be unbearable. Believers are still going to have money issues. Believers are still going to find that at times life can be unbearable.

But in the midst of all of this, knowing we can trust in God, knowing we can have our faith and hope in God, we can affirm this confession that is written in Philippians, which is best read in the King James Version of the Bible, "And the peace of God, which passes all understanding, shall keep your hearts and minds through Christ Jesus." Or, as we would say at a United Methodist communion service when we receive the ransomed blood of Jesus, "O Lamb of God, that takest away the sins of the world, grant us thy peace."

Becoming a Christian does not insulate us from the problems of life. But in a way that cannot be explained but only experienced spiritually, we do have an inner peace that passes all understanding.

It only took a day after the November 6 election for the hate mail to arrive. No chief executive had ever received

such an avalanche of correspondence, before or after the occupation of the Oval Office. The letters came north, crossing the Mason-Dixon Line, each calling for his execution by
gun, dagger, or hangman's noose. Some were more creative
than others. One letter had a fine sketch of the devil stab-
bing the president with a three-pronged fork, pitching him
into the fires of hell. If the letters were not message enough,
there was the shattering of the panes of glass at his Spring-
field home, irreparable signs of ill will. Abraham Lincoln
was troubled by these actions, forcefully stating that no "de-
cent man" could engage in such actions of hate and disdain.
Troubled enough by the letters, never casting aside the se-
riousness of the intent behind each, throughout his years in
the Oval Office he placed each letter in an envelope labeled
"Assassination."

We are still going to have that envelope labeled "Assassination" that gets thicker with each passing year of life as
our problems will never cease. But we can still live with the
faith and hope that sustained Lincoln during his trials and
tribulations when he said, "That I am not a member of any
Christian church is true; but I have never denied the truth of
the scriptures..." Abraham Lincoln never denied the truth of
the scriptures, giving him a trust, a faith, a hope, an assurance in God.

Our peace which passes all understanding comes from
reading and studying the Bible, and then believing in the
truth it conveys. Our peace which passes all understanding comes from attending worship, learning from others in
a Sunday school class, personal private home devotions,
participating in a small Christian fellowship group, and being active in the ministry and mission of this congregation.
These activities reinforce and inform that inner peace we felt
the first moment we accepted Jesus as our personal Savior.

Corrie ten Boom, who is best known for her book *The
Hiding Place*, was transferred to Ravensbruck Concentra-
tion Camp. The internment of this Hollander resulted from

her hiding people of the Jewish faith in her Christian home. As the women entered the camp they were taken to a shower room where they were ordered to undress. Their clothes and all their personal belongings were to be confiscated. Corrie had a Bible with her, without which she knew she could not survive the coming ordeal. Disrobing, she received a prison dress, under which she hid her Bible.

Two guards stood at the exit from the shower room, frisking each woman as she left. Desperate, helpless, Corrie prayed, "Lord, cause Your angels to surround me; the guards must not see me." A sense of peace came over Corrie. She walked relaxed and with ease past the guards, almost as if she was invisible. With the assurance that comes from prayer, Corrie ten Boom knew the steadfast love and faithfulness of God.

Having come to know Jesus as our Savior, we have also come to know that we are surrounded by angels.

1 Peter 2:19-25
Easter 4

Professional Angel

Marie Curie was devoted to science, determined to discover the medical possibilities for radiation. Working with radium slowly affected her health. Curie would often become ill, a result of radiation sickness. Painful burning lesions would appear on her hands and face, caused by handling radioactive material. Eventually, her vision was impaired; the only way she continued to work was by wearing thick lensed glasses and taping large color coded signs on her laboratory instruments. Yet, through this painstaking effort, the x-ray and early treatments for cancer were discovered. Marie Curie, the winner of two Nobel prizes for discovering radium and radioactivity, died of radiation poisoning in the summer of 1934 at the age of 66.

In the closing months of her life, realizing she was ill, Marie Curie refused to cease from her labors. She summarized her attitude in a letter addressed to her sister: "Sometimes my courage fails me and I think I ought to stop working, live in the country and devote myself to gardening. But I am held by a thousand bonds, and I don't know whether, even by writing scientific books, I could live without the laboratory."

Marie Curie persevered because she was a doer; she felt held to her work by a thousand bonds. Christian, you are bound to the gospel a thousand times, called to be a faithful doer of the word.

Marie Curie was "held by a thousand bonds" to be of service to others. She employed her talents to heal people. She employed her talents to make society better. She employed her talents to offer people hope. This is the calling of a Christian, which is to be "held by a thousand bonds" to offer others a ministry of caring in their misery and protection against the tribulations that confront them.

In our lectionary reading for this morning, Peter began by discussing how Christians suffer unjustly as a witness to their faith. Those Christians who suffered martyrdom as a result of their Christian witness found comfort in Jesus who suffered on the cross for his devotion and obedience to God, his heavenly Father.

But Peter did not stop there as he discussed that many Christians suffer from just the ordinary daily problems of life. These Christians, who suffer daily from circumstances beyond their control, often turn to Jesus for comfort and protection.

Peter tells us that we have our solace in Jesus because he suffered on the cross on our behalf. Realizing that Jesus suffered and understands suffering and suffered voluntarily for us that we might know redemption, we can be comforted by Jesus' spiritual presence.

From our lectionary reading this morning, Peter offers us two names, two titles for Jesus, which will describe how Jesus comforts us during our times of trial and tribulation. Jesus is the shepherd of our souls and Jesus is the guardian of our souls. Peter wrote, "For you were going astray like sheep, but now you have returned to the shepherd and guardian of your souls."

Life is not all bad, but neither is it all good. There are many good and happy things in life. Most of us do not wake up each morning to foreboding misery. We find happiness in our families, both nuclear and extended. We also have those special friends who we play cards with and have backyard picnics with. We enjoy going to the public parks, to the zoo, to museums, and to the stadium to watch our favorite sporting team. There is that favorite restaurant that we frequently visit. We probably even find greater happiness in the fellowship of the church than in the worship service itself. Actually, it has been shown that adults attend Sunday school less for the lesson and more for the fellowship. Many people do enjoy their jobs and find their work to be very rewarding and satisfying. Add to this those hobbies we love and the hours we spend on them, and how time just seems to disappear as we are engulfed in doing that which we enjoy.

But, unfortunately, life is not all good. We have a tendency from the pulpit to describe life as one great holocaust. This can overlook the joys of life, but it does recognize the real suffering and trauma that individuals endure.

The Merriam-Webster Dictionary defines holocaust "as an event or situation in which many people are killed and many things are destroyed especially by fire." The word was always a part of our vocabulary, but it did not come to the forefront until the Nazis began the elimination of the Jewish population in the 1940s.

Yet, for all of us life is a holocaust to some degree. And because life can be our own personal holocaust, we seek Jesus who is the shepherd and guardian of our souls.

What is the holocaust — the fire — that daily consumes the joy of life? It can be financial insecurity. It can be loneliness. It can be illness. It can be family problems. It can be problems at work. It can be uncertainty about the future. It can be that decision we make never knowing what the right decision will be, of course until it is too late to make a change. It could be that we got into a bad relationship. It could be that we stepped over a societal boundary and have found our self in an uncompromising situation. There is no end the list of our problems, real and potential. There is no way to avoid our personal holocaust.

As we live daily in these fires of destruction we seek out Jesus who is both our shepherd and guardian.

Dr. James Dunn, returning home after caring for the wounded during the battle of Antietam, told his wife about the heroism of a woman whom he met for the first time. Her name was Clara Barton. Dr. Dunn related how this nurse performed battlefield surgery using only a pocket knife. He told of the time a bullet that passed through the sleeve of her coat as she served water to a stricken soldier. He could not comprehend her stoicism as she held patients who were enduring amputations absent of chloroform.

After describing the exploits of this remarkable woman, the physician asked his wife, "Now what do you think of Miss Barton?" Mrs. Dunn thoughtfully responded, "In my feeble estimation, General McClellan, with all his laurels, sinks into insignificance beside the true heroine of the age, the angel of the battlefield." From that day forward Clara Barton had a title, "Angel of the Battlefield." To most, her calling card was "Professional Angel."

Jesus is for us a professional angel who binds our wounds and soothes our souls. This is why we go to Jesus to quench the fiery problems that are destroying our lives. Jesus, the professional angel, is the good shepherd who will always find us a green pasture in which to graze. Jesus, our guardian, will protect us from predators as we graze.

But, Jesus does not work alone. Jesus needs an angelic chorus to sing with him hymns of mercy and solitude. Therefore, we as the church are to be angels of mercy. We are the nurse practitioners in the name of Jesus, ready to place a soothing salve on any wound, be it physical, emotional, or spiritual. As a battlefield is strewn with friend and foe alike, we are to make no distinctions to whom we offer assistance. We care for each, not just to the individual who wears our uniform, but in the name of Christ every uniform is a call for us to be an angel of mercy.

The concept of shepherding is prominent throughout the scriptures, always depicted with the concept of service. In the Old Testament God is portrayed as the shepherd of Israel. Moses, as a shepherd boy, employed the same talents in leading the sheep of his fold through the Exodus journey. This image is duplicated for so many of the great leaders of the Jewish people. The patriarchs Abraham, Isaac, and Jacob were shepherds. David acquired his skill as a shepherd to defeat Goliath. The task of the shepherd is one of servitude, which is to be embraced as a spiritual leader.

Books have been written on all of the tasks and skills of a shepherd and how they parallel the expectations of Christian discipleship. This has become most prominent in literature regarding Jesus. Having referred to himself as the Good Shepherd, Jesus underscored the significance of this imagery. This was then adopted by the first-century authors, most notably Peter and Paul, in highlighting the shepherding ministry of the church. Peter conveyed this message with these words from our Lectionary reading that I read earlier this morning, "For you were going astray like sheep, but now you have returned to the shepherd and guardian of your souls."

Compare a few central teachings of Jesus regarding a shepherding ministry along with the requirements of the occupation of being a shepherd, and we will articulate the meaning of a Christian's calling to sacrificial service. Recorded in the tenth chapter of John's gospel is the best overview that Jesus provides of his self-understanding of fulfilling the role of being the good shepherd.

A shepherd would remain with each sheep in his flock for a lifetime, developing an eight to nine year relationship. In that time the shepherd would come to know each sheep by name and the sheep would recognize its shepherd's voice, responding to none other. Regarding Jesus, "He calls his own sheep by name." The gospel teaches regarding Jesus, "The sheep follow him, for they know his voice." From this we can understand that Christian service is very personal and intimate.

A shepherd would always lead his flock, never following behind. We are told of Jesus, "He goes before them and the sheep follow him." The shepherd would be the first one to pass through dangerous mountain crevasses. The shepherd would know where the scarce grazing land could be found and where the few watering troughs were located. The shepherd knew how far the sheep could journey without becoming too weary, especially when the ewes were with young. The shepherd was a conscientious, knowledgeable, and benevolent leader.

Jesus said of himself, "I am the gate for the sheep." At night the sheep were always placed in an encircled closure. This could be a cave or a make shift corral of gathered bushes. There would only be one single opening, or gate. The shepherd would always sleep at the opening. A member of the flock could not escape without awakening the caretaker; an animal of prey could not enter without confronting the protector. Ministry requires constant vigilance. Ministry requires both a shepherd and a guardian.

As the sheep entered the encampment for the evening the shepherd would hold his rod low across the narrow entrance. Each sheep would therefore have to pass under the rod. In so doing, the shepherd could examine each one for injury. That is the picture that Ezekiel presented when he heard God say, "I will make you pass under the rod." It is a portrait of God's loving care for his people. The same devotion is displayed by Jesus throughout his public ministry. We are to be compassionate, sincerely concerned about each individual within our flock.

It was dangerous work, not tranquil as recalled from our children's Sunday school literature. The work requires a guardian. The wolf, hyena, leopard, panther, bear, and lion were the animals that preyed upon the sheep. The rod and the sling were the shepherd's only means to ward off these vicious creatures. Thieves and brigands were common foes, often attacking a shepherd in small gangs. Jesus the guardian of his flock said, "The good shepherd lays down his life for his sheep." In service to the Lord, there is no ceiling to the sacrifice that may be expected. Thankfully, most of us need not endure such a burden, but if confronted it is expected.

Jesus said of himself, "I am the good shepherd." This is one of the most forthright statements Jesus made regarding his earthly pilgrimage. It is one that we must take to heart and emulate to the best of our ability. It is not the image of a passive individual, for ministry requires courage. It compels perseverance and courage, always remaining attuned to the assigned task of guardian. This is balanced with a gentle spirit of a shepherd, perceptive of the physical, emotional and spiritual depravity from which many in our flock may be suffering.

In Latin the word "pastor" means "shepherd." It came from the same root word *pascere* which means to "feed" or "pasture." A pastor is an individual who shepherds others, caring for their most basic needs. Traditionally in the church the position of pastor is rightfully held by the ordained clergy, though, this does not preclude the laity from being pastoral in relationship to others.

As shepherds, let us go forth with the charge of John Wesley, the founder of Methodism in the eighteenth century, with these words of ministry embedded in our souls: "I look on all the world as my parish; thus far I mean, that, in whatever part of it I am, I judge it meet, right, and my bounden duty, to declare unto all that are willing to hear, the glad tidings of salvation."

Our world is found in our place of work, our neighborhood, our church, our friends, our family — this is what we look upon as our parish. As Wesley said, "that, in whatever part of it I am, I judge it meet, right, and my bounden duty, to declare unto all that are willing to hear, the glad tidings of salvation."

1 Peter 2:2-10
Easter 5

Didache

The first-century church took seriously the need to educate new converts about the meaning of Jesus and Christianity. The earliest formal educational tool was called "The Teaching of the Twelve Apostles," also known as the *Didache*, which in Greek means "teaching." It was compiled at the first Apostolic Council convened in Jerusalem in the year 51. The proceedings of the council are recorded in the fifteenth chapter of the book of Acts in the New Testament. The gathering was called to give direction to the church, less than twenty years after the death of Jesus. The *Didache* was the first book written for the formal instruction for new converts. It is most prominently known for establishing the theological doctrine of "The Two Ways." Divided into three sections, the *Didache* contained Christian lessons, rituals for baptism and the Eucharist, and church organization.

A partial reading of *Didache* will provide us with an understanding of what and how the *Didache* taught. The book begins by discussing "The Two Ways," the way of life and the way of death.

The opening verse reads: "Two ways there are, one of life and one of death, but there is a great difference between the two ways. The way of life is indeed this: First, you will love the God who made you; secondly, 'you will love your neighbor as yourself.' Now all the things that you do not want to have happen to you, you too do not do these to one another." The way of life is further discussed, and then the book moves on to discuss the way of death.

This section, the way of death, begins with these words, "Now the way of death is this: First of all, it is evil and full

113

of curses: murders, adulteries, strong desires, unlawful sex acts, thefts, idolatries, magic acts, sorceries, robberies, false testimonies, hypocrisies, two-heartedness, deceit, arrogance, badness, assumptions, greed, shameful speech, jealousy, an overbearing nature, loftiness, pride; persecutors of good; hating truth, loving falsehood; not knowing the reward of what is right, not clinging to good, nor to just judgment, watching not for good but for evil. Far from these people are meekness and endurance. They love worthless things, perusing revenge...." The book continues to describe a pagan lifestyle.

The purpose of the *Didache* was to instruct converts on how to forsake their former lifestyles and now live as a Christian. Many of the self-centered actions of debauchery listed in the ways of death were condoned in the Greek society. It was a major social and educational effort for the early church leaders to convince converts to surrender these evil ways that only lead to spiritual death and accept the Christian attributes that puts one on the path that leads to spiritual life.

Immediately after the resurrection of Jesus the only scripture that Christians possessed was the Hebrew Bible. Gathering together they would read from this book and then preach a sermon in which Christ became the central message from the verses read from the Jewish scriptures. This sufficed until the church expanded into Gentile communities whose residents had no knowledge of the Hebrew scriptures. This necessitated the writing of additional Christian material to supplement the *Didache* for learning purposes. It was also at this time that the letters of Paul, James, John, Peter, and many other authors whose epistles were never canonized circulated among the churches. The foremost purpose of these letters was instructional. The *Didache*, preaching from the Hebrew Bible, and the letters of church leaders conveyed the lessons of Christianity to the parishioners of the first century church.

From our lectionary reading this morning, Peter began this section of his letter by discussing how important it was for Christians to learn the doctrines of the church. Peter then told the readers that knowledge was important because Christians collectively, not individually, will "be built into a spiritual house," which is the church. Peter then said that educated Christians, who as a community of believers compose the membership of the church, have the responsibility of "proclaiming the mighty acts" of Jesus.

Peter wrote, "Like newborn infants, long for the pure spiritual milk, so that they may grow into salvation." These new converts are longing for pure spiritual milk. They want to learn. They look upon learning as a joyous exercise. They know that only by learning the doctrines of the church will they be able to grow and mature as Christians. They have taken their new life in Christ so seriously that they have an unquenchable desire to learn as much about Jesus as possible.

This desire to learn was a symbolic part of some baptismal ceremonies. After the new converts were baptized and given a white robe to wear, symbolizing their new unblemished life in Christ, they were given milk to drink as if they were little children. This symbolic act of drinking milk demonstrated that they needed to be nourished to grow from newborn converts into full adulthood in their religious understanding of Christianity.

So the question becomes how seriously do we take educating ourselves as Christians? So the question becomes do we look upon the learning of Christian doctrine as a joyful endeavor?

There are many educational fountains that we can drink milk from, but we need to choose more than one. The first fountain of course is the daily reading our Bibles. It would help if we had a Bible with a commentary printed on the page and in addition to this actually purchasing a Bible commentary. Commentaries provide so much information from culture to theology to word meanings to the context in which the verse is used to parallel passages to historical setting. All of this information takes us on a journey right into the Bible verse on the very day it was originally written.

Attending a small study group that meets regularly allows for discussion and learning from the insights of others. It is for this same reason we should attend Sunday school. Listening to a sermon can inform and inspire us, but it falls short as being as productive as belonging to an educational group.

We need to read other Christian academic material. We need to put on the shelf authors who only pretend to be scholars such as Rick Warren, Joel Osteen, Tim LeHaye, Joyce Meyers, Robert Schuller, and many others who are more self-help authors and populists than academics.

There are some excellent theologians who wrote books whose theology is orthodox and are easy to understand. But since they lived in the halls of universities and were not seen on television standing in their megachurch we are not as aware of them or we discard them as being too intellectual. But they are not too intellectual and can be easily read. Some of these authors are C.S. Lewis, Philip Yancey, Dietrich Bonhoeffer, Pope Francis, Harold Kushner, Leonard Sweet, Tony Campolo, William Temple, and many other scholars who should take up residence on your book shelf.

And we ought to read the writings of those who founded denominations like Martin Luther, John Wesley, John Calvin, George Fox, who are some of the great writers that have set things in motion and influence our doctrines today.

Beyond reading there are also some great educational videos by PBS and the History Channel, but stay away from Hollywood movies that will fabricate anything in order to entertain.

It is our responsibility to become educated and informed Christians. Education has always been an important mandate of the church. The importance ascribed to being a Christian teacher is outlined in the *Constitutions of the Holy Fathers, Book VII*, written in the fourth century, which states, "That it is our duty to esteem our Christian teachers above our parents — the former being the means of our well-being, the other only of our being." Not only are we to take on the responsibility of learning, we are to take on the responsibility of teaching others.

We must be ready to give some milk to that convert wearing the white robe who just came up and out of the baptismal water.

That individual we just gave milk to and desires more milk for nurturing, he or she is now a part of the Christian community. Peter wrote that we are "built into a spiritual house," that is the church. Peter wrote that this spiritual house is a corporate community saying it is composed of "a chosen race, a royal priesthood, a holy nation, God's own people."

These are metaphors that Peter took from the Old Testament that referred to Israel and Peter declared the church had become God's new holy nation. In the church there is a new promised land of grace and redemption. The church offers a new covenant, not based on Jewish legalism, but on the redemption offered by the grace of Christ on the cross.

If you take a moment to look around the sanctuary you will see your brothers and sisters in Christ, your Christian family. The biblical scholar C.E.B. Cranfield once wrote, "The free-lance Christian, who would be a Christian but is too superior to belong to the visible church upon earth in one of its forms, is simply a contradiction in terms."

You cannot be a free-lance Christian. You must belong to a Christian community. I know many people say they do not need the church to be religious, and that would be a correct statement. But what they don't say is that absent from the church they lack the ability to learn and mature in the faith, and they forsake the institution that promotes Christian ministry and missions. Yes, they can be a Christian apart from the church, but they are only pretending if they say they are promoting the evangelical mission of the church.

In August 29, 2005, Hurricane Katrina crashed upon the city of New Orleans. Five years later, though many of the buildings and bridges have been rebuilt, the emotional damage remained rampant. Because homes were lost and families were displaced, many even separated one from another, the emotional trauma it created had not been healed by the year 2010. A study, led by David Abramson of Columbia University, confirmed that the physiological problems the hurricane created have yet to be resolved.

The study was focused on the children of the city, those who returned and those who are still displaced. Abramson said, "If children are the bellwethers of recovery, then the social systems supporting affected Gulf Coast populations are still far from having recovered from Hurricane Katrina." He said, "Children are a bit of a canary in a coal mine in that they really represent a failure or a dysfunction of many, many other systems in the community."

David Abramson's study can be applied to the church. The church can only function when the systems that comprise it are working in harmony. The church can only function when the membership cooperates as a community.

This is Peter's message that the church is a "spiritual house" that is absent of free-lance Christians. According to Peter the church is a community described as "a chosen race, a royal priesthood, a holy nation, God's own people."

When the church is a community comprised of Christians who have learned the Bible and orthodox theology, then it will fulfill its mission of "proclaiming the mighty acts of Jesus who has called people out of darkness into his marvelous light."

The mission of the church is really to teach "the two ways" of the *Didache*, the way of life and the way of death. The church is to teach the way out of darkness and the way into marvelous light. We are to share with others the mighty acts of Jesus. We are to help people understand grace and forgiveness, and most importantly of all, we are to lead people into accepting Jesus Christ as their Lord and Savior.

We do this as a supportive community. We all have different spiritual gifts that when combined in the Christian community have the force of nuclear proportions. It is a joy as we look around this sanctuary knowing that together we can do as Jesus said, "Very truly I tell you, whoever believes in me will do the works I have been doing, and they will do even greater things than these." Look around the sanctuary and ponder how we as a community, "a holy nation," can do the mighty works of Jesus.

On June 18, 1983, Sally Ride became the first American woman in space as a crew member on Space Shuttle Challenger. In elementary school she became excited about space travel as she watched the Mercury space program on television. It was an excitement that was contagious among all her classmates, both boys and girls. She said, "When I was growing up science was cool. So we need to make science cool again."

Ride was particularly concerned about the lack of interest that girls have in science. Middle-school girls want to be popular, and going to an astronomy class is not a peer enhancing proposition. Further, what young lady wants to aspire to be a scientist when they are depicted as, in Ride's words, "some geeky-looking guy who looks like Einstein, wears a lab coat and pocket protector"?

In order to change the image of scientists from being geeky to being normal, family centered individuals who pursue a career of exciting adventures and discoveries, she started the Sally Ride Science Academy. The academy shares with teachers methods to present math and science in creative, innovated and exciting ways. In this way science can become, in Ride's words, more "real and relevant" to the students.

It is our calling as the teachers of the Bible and the community that has built a spiritual house to make the gospel real and relevant.

The Last Pew

Immersion in water was always a sacred rite in Judaism. Jewish synagogues, whenever possible, were built next to sources of water. The Jewish baptistry would often be two pools connected by a channel to allow pure water to flow into the baptistry. The baptistry had to hold a minimum of 75 gallons of water to allow an adult to be fully immersed.

After the resurrection of Jesus, Christians adopted the ritual of baptism as the entrance rite into the church. For the early church to participate in the ritual of baptism was to participate in the resurrection of Jesus, and to have a new life that is now lived in Christ.

This was symbolically represented that when an individual went beneath the water and came up out of the water, it symbolized dying to one's self and living for Christ. For the first 200 years Christians were baptized in lakes, rivers and ponds, wherever a source of water could be found. But in the third century, when churches were being built, the church adopted the practice using a baptistry for baptism.

The earliest known baptistry is located in a house church at Dura-Europos, and is dated in the year 240. The layout of this baptistry is representative of all baptistries of this time period, though over the centuries they did evolve into different configurations.

The baptistry at Dura-Europos measured five feet four inches in length, by three feet four inches in width, and three feet one inch in depth. There was a ledge to allow the person being baptized to lean over to be immersed. There was a canopy over the baptistry that had painted on it a blue sky with stars. On the west end of the room was a painting of

Jesus as the good shepherd with sheep. Also on that canvas was a very small painting of Adam and Eve with the serpent in the garden. On the east wall was a painting of the women approaching the empty tomb. Also on that painting is a picture of Jesus and Peter walking on water. The baptistry was octagonal in shape because in biblical numerology, the number eight was the number that symbolized immortality.

The symbolism of the baptistry is very important for us in understanding the meaning of baptism for the early church. The night canvas represents the God of creation. Jesus as the Good Shepherd tells us that he will be our provider and protector. The image of Adam and Eve shows us that we are now free from sin. Jesus and Peter walking on water shows us that Jesus does perform miracles. The women running towards the empty tomb declares the resurrection of Jesus. The octagonal shape professes that with our baptism we have eternal life.

Peter in our lectionary reading for this morning wrote that Noah and eight people aboard the ark were saved through water. These eight individuals were Noah and his wife, his three sons Shem, Ham, and Japheth, and their three wives. By discussing Noah, Peter was saying baptism brings safety to Christians because a baptized person lives in the spirit of Christ.

Reflecting on the story of Noah and applying the analogy to Christian baptism Peter wrote, "And baptism, which Noah prefigured, now saves you, not as a removal of dirt from your body, but as an appeal to God for a good conscience, through the resurrection of Jesus Christ."

With our baptism we know that we have salvation. With our baptism we know that our sins have been forgiven. With our baptism we know that we now live a new life free of debauchery. With our baptism we now live a life blessed by the spirit of Christ which gives us a sense of security.

Because our baptism is such a meaningful experience for us, Peter says that once we are baptized it is our desire to become witnesses for Jesus. Peter wrote, "Always be ready to make your defense to anyone who demands from you an accounting for the hope that is in you." Making a defense of your faith also means sharing your faith. It means sharing the hope that is in you. In other words, it means sharing what Jesus Christ means to you.

Sharing our faith is something that most people are very hesitant to do. This is understandable and should not be criticized from the pulpit.

The reason for this is people fear that they do not know the Bible well enough to discuss it. This goes beyond the fear of being biblically illiterate, but also the fear of being embarrassed by not knowing the Bible better.

This embarrassment extends to being asked a religious question that we cannot answer.

People are unsure of the doctrines of the denomination they belong to, and they feel trapped by a lack of knowledge.

Individuals are also unsure of their own religious experience. Though being a Christian is a real and vital part of their life, they don't feel comfortable in sharing their story with others.

In addition to not knowing what to say, there is also the problem of knowing when and where to witness and to whom one should witness.

It may appear that there is no one to witness to because everyone that we know is already a Christian and there is a lot of truth to this. Most of us don't really know any true atheists or agnostics or just plain unbelievers. But, there are people out there with whom to share the gospel message.

There are the individuals who are members of our own congregation who have stopped coming to church. They are certainly a group of people that we should have a conversation with. In fact, it is wrong not to go to them since they are a part of this congregational family. The same goes for others we know who have stopped attending another church.

We should go to them with a sense of encouragement to once again get involved in the fellowship of believers.

There is always the sorrowful situation when a great tragedy has come upon an individual or family. We fear going to them again out of an embarrassment of not knowing what properly to say. But, we forget that the mere fact that we went to them is our witness, even if we just sit in silence with them.

It is difficult to witness at our place of employment, this I know and realize. But, there will always be that moment of casual conversation when sharing what Jesus means to you could be helpful to a coworker.

Then, there are always those spontaneous moments with a neighbor, or as we are walking in the park, or as we are attending our exercise class or some other activity, when that casual conversation becomes an opportunity to share what Jesus means to me.

And witnessing what Jesus means to you personally and being able to express it will always be the best witness. Being able to articulate your own faith story with conviction and sincerity will compensate for any lack of knowledge you have about the Bible or those tough theological questions that you cannot give an answer to.

But, in all of this we must always remember the instruction of Peter when he wrote, "Always be ready to make a defense to make your defense to anyone who demands from you an accounting for the hope that is in you." We must always be ready to witness. So the question becomes, are you ready?

It is interesting, and most helpful, that Peter does offer some suggestions on how to witness. Peter's few words do not compare to lengthy books we find in Christian book stores, but I wonder if his few words actually say more than all those published pages combined.

In discussing how we are to witness Peter wrote that we are not to be "intimidated." Peter said that we are to offer the "hope that is in us," Peter wrote that we are to witness with "gentleness." Peter wrote that we are to witness with "reverence." And Peter wrote that we are to witness with a "clear conscious."

Peter wrote that we are not to be intimidated in our witness. There is no reason for us to apologize for being a Christian. There will be some individuals who will argue with us and present questions and opinions that we will not be able to adequately counter. This is not reason enough to begin to doubt or make concessions for what we believe.

Peter wrote that when we witness we are to offer the hope that is in us. The central message of the Bible is a message of hope. It is a message of always having the possibility of a new beginning. It is the message that no matter how difficult life becomes we have hope because we know that Jesus is watching over us. Our hope also comes from our church family who we know will support us and provide for us in a time of need. And of course, the ultimate message of hope is the resurrection that brought us forth into eternal life. It is a hope that no matter how despairing life becomes, we will one day be safe and secure in heaven. When we witness we share this hope that sustains our lives from day to day.

Peter wrote that we witness with gentleness. We are never arrogant. We are never boastful. And certainly we never demean or humiliate someone because they do not believe. When we witness we are gentle, kind, and respectful so the person to whom we are speaking with does not feel demoralized.

Peter wrote that when we witness we do so with reverence. We witness in a manner that is respectful of God.

Peter wrote that when we witness we do so with a clear conscious. A clear conscious means that we witness absent of a sense of guilt. We realize that we are all sinners and that we are not perfect. No one is perfect except Jesus.

I think that this is one of the great burdens placed upon clergy. People say they do not expect their pastor to be sinless, yet in their judgement they disavow the pastor from any possibility of being a human being with frailties. But, for us in the congregation to witness with a clear conscious is to say I am a sinner, I am not perfect, but I do struggle daily to be the best Christian possible. And this is true for your pastor as well.

I think Peter's short outline on how to witness should encourage all of us. Peter did not focus on how much we know about the Bible. Peter's focus was on how we present ourselves as loving and caring individuals.

There are many forms of evangelism, but the one that is most effective and most sincere is called relational evangelism. Relational evangelism is often defined as "earning the right to be heard." It comes from building an intentional relationship with an individual, who could be a family member, a friend, a neighbor, a participant at your club, a coworker. We earn credibility with them by being a friend, by developing a meaningful relationship with them. Then you patiently wait for a spiritual conversation to come about. When the topic of faith comes up, you've earned the right to share your story of Jesus. You have "earned the right to be heard."

Relational evangelism is the most effective evangelical practice to bring someone to Christ and into the church, which is the Body of Christ. Evangelist Luis Palau's research shows that 75% of all those who come to Christ do so through a relationship with a saved friend, relative, or coworker. The Institute of American Church Growth reports an even higher percentage, with almost 90% of the 14,000 Christians polled saying they came to Christ through "a friend or relative who invested in a relationship with them."

Peter's outline for witnessing is really an outline for relational evangelism. It is relational because we are gentle and kind. It is relational because we are not judgmental or demeaning. And most importantly, we share, as a friend, our story of conversion and what Jesus means to us in our daily lives. We share with an individual with whom we have developed a friendly, trusting, and respectful relationship.

It was a difficult day for a man desperate for work. After serving ten years in the United States Navy, and a few more years working in warehouses, he decided to become an actor. Attending acting school when he could, he finally got his chance to try out for his first movie role. When he arrived on the set, there were forty people before him. The casing director told him to "Go and lose yourself for a couple of hours." With only fifteen cents in his pocket he walked down New York City's Fifth Avenue. He came to St. Patrick's Cathedral and felt the need to climb the wide stone steps and enter the church. There he sat in the last pew and offered this prayer: "Please, Father, I need the work. If you can possibly help me, I would appreciate it very much." He returned to the studio and was cast for his first movie role in *The Whistle at Eaton Falls*. Thus began the acting career of Ernest Borgnine. This miracle in the last pew of St. Patrick's Cathedral not only began Ernest Borgnine acting career, but it also became his personal story, his personal witness of what Jesus means to him.

Let us go forth and share our story — our story of what Jesus means to us.

Te Deum

The Fourth Ecumenical Council, also known as the Council of Chalcedon, was a church council held from October to November, in the year 451. Chalcedon is an ancient maritime town in a region of the Roman Empire in northwest Asia Minor. At this council the delegates composed the Latin hymn of praise *Te Deum*, with the English translation being "A Song of the Church." These several stanzas refer to the enthronement of Jesus and his power over creation:

> *Thou art the King of Glory, O Christ,*
> *Thou art the everlasting Son: of the Father.*
> *Thou art the everlasting Son: of the Father.*
> *When thou tookest upon thee to deliver man: thou didst*
> *not abhor the Virgin's womb.*
> *When thou hadst overcome the sharpness of death:*
> *thou didst open the kingdom of heaven to all believers.*
> *Thou sittest at the right hand of God: in the glory of the*
> *Father.*

Paul confesses that Christ is the king of glory who has opened heaven to all believers. Paul recognizes in his letter the enthronement of Jesus Christ, who now, sitting at the right hand of God, that everything in heaven and on earth are under his sovereign rule. What Paul confessed in the first century, the church continued to confess in the fifth century, as we still confess today in the twenty-first century.

A hymn written by the church in the fifth century reflects the confession Paul made in the first century, as recorded in our lectionary reading this morning, when Paul wrote, "God put this power to work in Christ when he raised him from the dead and seated him at his right hand in heavenly places, far above all rule and authority and power and dominion, and above every name that is named, not only in this age but in the age to come."

In Greek society the pagan gods and idols that were worshiped have lost any authority once ascribed to them because Christ is enthroned at the right hand of God. Kings, pontiffs, and sovereigns have lost their power as they are under the authority of the enthroned Christ. Merchants have lost their power because they reside beneath the throne of Christ. This certainly does not mean that these individuals could not do mean and illicit things this day, but it does mean that for some of them, now, and for all at the eschaton, they will be totally subservient to the Lord of the cosmos.

But, Paul recognized that the enthroned Christ exercises his power through the church. The church as the Body of Christ is the greatest title that could be bestowed upon the church and is a common theme in the Bible, especially for Paul who wrote Ephesians. Paul often wrote about Jesus being the head of the church and the church being the Body of Christ. And Paul discussed how the human body was made up of many different parts, such as eyes, ears, hands, and feet, and each cannot do the work of the other, but synchronized together they accomplish on earth the work of the head, who is Christ.

Paul discussed this concept in more detail in his letter to the church in Corinth, and the theme is repeated in our reading this morning when Paul wrote, "And he has put all things under his feet and has made him the head over all things for the church, which is his body."

The church now becomes the hands and feet and mouth of Jesus on earth. This is a calling that everyone sitting in the pews of this sanctuary this morning must take very seriously. The scriptures tell us that Jesus expects you — the Christian — to continue his earthly mission. This is not a calling that we can forsake. We must be willing to minister in the name of Jesus.

I like this passage from Luke. It is perhaps the best description of what the calling of the church is when Jesus quotes Isaiah to describe his ministry:

> *"The Spirit of the Lord is on me, because he has anointed me to proclaim good news to the poor. He has sent me to proclaim freedom for the prisoners and recovery of sight for the blind, to set the oppressed free, to proclaim the year of the Lord's favor."*

We could not have a more descriptive statement than this to outline the ministry and mission of the church.

The Christian community — the church — is Jesus in the world today. If we falter in fulfilling our calling as disciples of Jesus, then we have denied Jesus the opportunity to minister in our communities. If we are obedient in following the teachings of the scriptures then we can make Jesus present among the poor, the prisoners, the blind, the oppressed, and introduce individuals to the grace of our Lord.

Henry Gerecke is not a household name; yet, he had one of the most significant callings in the history of the church. He was the chaplain to 21 Nazi war criminals during the Nuremberg Trials, and shepherded five of the most notorious Nazis to the gallows. Gerecke was a Lutheran pastor from Missouri, who was fluent in German. He volunteered as a chaplain to serve in the Army in 1943 when the military was desperate for men to serve in that capacity. His war time duties took him to Dachau where he witnessed the Nazi atrocities of the Holocaust. At the time he was unaware of his future role.

During the Nuremberg Trials, those overseeing the proceedings learned of a German speaking chaplain. They asked Gerecke to take on the role as the minister to those accused of crimes against humanity. Gerecke accepted. During his counseling sessions, he would only offer Holy Communion

131

to those men who were truly penitent and confessed their faith in Jesus Christ. Only four sentenced to hang met Gerecke's standard and received the Eucharist. One unrepentant Nazi officer said, "This Jesus that you always speak of, to me he is just another smart Jew."

After the war, Gerecke was criticized for ministering to the monsters of the Third Reich. Gerecke responded that he considered his calling to the Nuremberg defendants to be a mission.

We are called to serve the Lord in our present position in life. We do not have to be a clergyperson to be called into service. Each of us is an ambassador for the Lord in whatever is our present capacity in life.

James Cash Penney was a businessman when he opened his first store in 1902 in Kemmerer, Wyoming. He named the store J.C. Penney. Committing himself to the highest ethical standards possible, he based his business on biblical principles. Of these, the most important principle for him was the Golden Rule.

Jesus placed no restrictions on whom was called into ministry. He summoned both a fisherman and a tax collector. The message for us as a clergyperson, as a business person, as a homemaker, or as a community worker is that we all have a special calling and a special place to serve.

Martin Luther, the founder of Protestantism in the sixteenth century, put forth the theological doctrine of the "priesthood of all believers." It is the declaration that everyone is a priest. Everyone has a special role to play in the service of the church.

For all of us gathered together in this sanctuary, each one us brings a unique gift to the ministry of this church. And each gift complements the other. This is what makes us a congregation. This is what makes us the priesthood of all believers. This is what makes us the Body of Christ.

Since we are the Body of Christ working in harmony with one another it is time to examine the contribution you can make to the ministry and mission of the church. Some of you have already found your place in the body of servants, others are still seeking a place, and yet there are some who have not looked at all.

In several places in the New Testament we are provided with a list of the gifts of the spirit. These are spiritual gifts bestowed upon Christians that accentuate their special calling in ministry. It is possible to have more than one spiritual gift. I like the list provided by Paul in Romans for it seems to be the most relevant to our congregation today. Paul writes this as his list: "if it is serving, then serve; if it is teaching, then teach; if it is to encourage, then give encouragement; if it is giving, then give generously; if it is to lead, do it diligently; if it is to show mercy, do it cheerfully."

Of course this list is not exhaustive. There are many other spiritual gifts that do not appear on this list. But, the list should get you thinking of where your place is in the Body of Christ and how you may best contribute to the ministry and mission of the church.

We must be aware that these gifts are not confined to the church. Your spiritual gift can manifest itself as you are involved with your family and friends, in your community, at your place of employment, and at your favorite social activity. The most important thing to remember is whether we are working in the church or elsewhere in the community we are doing the ministry of Jesus.

To be a disciple Paul emphasized the need to learn about Jesus. The better we understand the teaching and ministry of Jesus the more prepared we will be to be a representative of Jesus in ministry. Paul wrote, "I pray that the God of our Lord Jesus Christ, the Father of glory, may give you a spirit of wisdom and revelation as you come to know him."

May we increase in our wisdom as we come to know Jesus. Because the greater our wisdom, the greater our understanding we have of Jesus then the better we will be in preforming our tasks as Christian disciples. We need to make an effort to study the Bible and attend church educational groups so we can increase in our wisdom.

"Tata Jesus is bangala declared the reverend every Sunday at the end of his sermon. 'More and more, mistrusting his interpreters, he tried to speak for himself in Kikongo. He threw back his head and shouted these words in the sky, while the attendees sat scratching themselves in wonder. "Bangala" means something precious and dear. But the way he pronounced it, it meant the poisonwood tree. So he preached,' Praise the Lord, hallelujah, my friends! For Jesus will make you itch like nobody's business."

This paragraph was written by Barbara Kingsolver in her book *The Poisonwood Bible*. It is the story of the Price family who pilgrimaged from Bethlehem, Georgia to the Belgian Congo as missionaries in 1959. Reverend Nathan Price, autocratic and self-righteous, was an old school missionary who firmly believed that the gospel of salvation coupled with Americanization was the only viable means to transform a tribal people into a civilized society. Aghast rather than respectful of their customs, not only was he unable to speak their language, but he failed to comprehend the significance and beauty of an intricate social system that he could only view as barbaric.

As an uncompromising Baptist minister, Price held firm that salvation required baptism, and baptism necessitated being immersed. The only water suitable for the sacrament of repentance was the river. Repeatedly the villagers would flee rather than flock when summoned to the river bank for baptism.

It took many a month for Price to learn that several children had been devoured by crocodiles that lurked in those forbidden murky river waters. Inflexible, even with this discovery, he remained relentless in his pursuit to baptize converts in the hellish river. What well-meaning parent would place a son or daughter in such danger for any god;

especially one whose joyful hallelujahs could bring upon them an unforgiving rash?

To understand and to be understood we need wisdom. Absent of wisdom our ministry will be a folly that only produces an unforgiving rash.